THE SKIP WILKINS' STORY

The Real Race

BY SKIP WILKINS AND JOSEPH DUNN

TYNDALE HOUSE
Publishers, Inc.
Wheaton, Illinois

It's an impossible task to mention all of the families, friends, and people who have helped me in my life and with this book.

I am grateful to all of them and I hope that they are proud of what they have helped one person to do with his life.

Skip Wilkins

Bible quotations from The New International Version of *The Holy Bible,* copyright 1978 by the New York International Bible Society, are used by permission of Zondervan Corporation.

Bible quotations from *The New English Bible,* copyright 1961, 1970 by the Delegates of the Oxford University Press and the Syndics of the Cambridge University Press, are used by permission.

First printing, trade paper edition, February 1987
Library of Congress Catalog Card Number 85-50775
ISBN 0-8423-5283-X
Copyright 1981 by Skip Wilkins and Joseph Dunn
Printed in the United States of America

To my family
To my wife
And all to the
glory of God

Contents

The Real Race

In a race there are many runners,
but only one gets the prize.
The runner goes into strict training
for this race and runs with his
mind set on winning, only for a prize
that will fade away.
But the real race is life.
I run this race with a commitment
to God and a determined faith, so there
is no chance of being disqualified.
For this prize will not fade away,
but will last forever.

Skip Wilkins

Part I

Part I

1

The Bottom of the Lake

The Monday after graduating from high school Skip Wilkins was up early for work. During school he had worked part-time as a stock clerk in a department store. Now he was starting his first day as a sales clerk in the store's china department.

Gary O'Brien, a surfing buddy, stopped by the store in mid-morning to invite Skip to go waterskiing that afternoon.

"Why skiing?" Skip asked. "The surf's got to be great this afternoon. The wind's been out of the west all night. The waves ought to be really shaped."

Gary left. When he returned, his persistence and the two attractive girls with him changed Skip's mind.

Skip had never skied on Lake Joyce. The lake was extremely small, but he assumed that it opened into Chesapeake Bay and that they would ski in the bay.

"Boy, what a boat," Skip said as he walked down to the dock. The boat had an 80-horsepower Mercury tilted out of the water on the stern. It was built for speed and pulling skiers. Skip was glad now that he had decided not to go surfing. The afternoon was going to be great.

In fact, he was an excellent water skier. He felt more natural behind a speeding boat—pulling off to the sides and cutting the ski's edge into the water to throw up huge rooster tails—than on a surfboard.

The boat pulled away from the dock and followed the shoreline for a short distance to the right, heading toward a point. Skip thought the entrance to the bay would be around the point, but Gary stopped the boat and idled the motor.

"Skip, go ahead."

Debbie was getting her skis to throw over the side. Skip dropped the slalom ski into the water. Both were quickly ready to go. Skip nodded his head and motioned forward with his left hand.

Gary eased the throttle forward slowly until the tow ropes stretched out and became taut, then he gave the engine more throttle until Skip and Debbie, still in a crouch, broke the surface, found their balance, and stood upright.

The boat rapidly picked up speed and cleared the point. Skip could see that what lay ahead wasn't the entrance to the bay. It was just a large cove. He thought how small the lake was compared to Currituck Sound where he normally skied.

The boat followed the shoreline of the cove, making a wide turn for a run in the other direction. Skip, on the outward side behind the boat, cut close to the shore, then out again.

As the boat made its run down the far shoreline, Skip pulled back on the two handles and leaned hard to his right, almost a 45-degree angle to the surface. The shift of weight quickly sent him wide to the right of the stern, close to the shore. He shifted his weight now to the left and cut across the wake of the boat, coming out of the water in the single ski as he hit the wake. He was quickly across the stern and wide to the left of the boat, outside of Debbie, whose wide smile said she was impressed.

He swung back, crossing the wake and swinging again wide to the right and close to shore. He was closing fast on a line of rocks just offshore and he began to shift his weight again in order to pull away from the dangerous area.

He felt a jolt. He sensed incredible speed. The rest happened too suddenly for his mind to comprehend.

His ski had hit a rock just below the surface. Skip was jerked out of the ski and up into the air before instinct, or fear, made him drop the tow bar. It was as if his body had been thrown from a sling. He was hurtling through space, somersaulting like a football thrown end over end.

Then he slammed into the lake.

His first thought was that some huge force had raised him up by his shoulders and smashed him, like a piece of glass, against concrete. The image of broken bones, crushed so small that they provided no more shape to his body, flashed across his mind. Then it was gone.

He opened his eyes. He was looking at water, water that had been stirred by something. A stick, a hand. The water was churning and sandy. He could see bubbles rising. Above him, within easy reach, perhaps a foot, maybe more, he saw leaves, then grassy stalks stretching upward, to either side of his head.

He was under water.

He couldn't move.

He couldn't feel anything.

Strangely, his mind registered no panic. He knew that he was hurt, perhaps seriously. His only thought was that he might never play football again. Then he closed his eyes.

He felt a ring of air around his nose. But that was all he could feel. Then he heard the boat's motor, muffled by the water. The sound came closer and closer. He could make out voices, but he couldn't understand what the voices were saying. He had the sensation of bobbing like a log in the water, only his face above the surface. He couldn't focus his mind on anything around him.

He wondered if he were dying.

Or if he were already dead.

"Skip, you all right? What's wrong?"

"I'm hurt. I'm hurt real bad," he said.

"You're probably just stunned. You'll be all right. Just hold on. We'll get you up on shore. We're only a few feet away."

"No. Don't. Don't move me. I'm hurt bad." Skip could hear the two girls. They were becoming hysterical. They started to cry.

"Get a rescue squad," Skip said.

He heard movement in the water. Someone was leaving.

Skip turned his head slightly to the right to look at Gary, standing in the shallow water and leaning over him. Skip's right arm was draped over Gary's shoulder. Skip couldn't feel it. The arm was limp and awkward looking. He tried to remove it, to bring it back down by his side in the water. It stayed on Gary's shoulder. He tried again. This time he told himself to move his arm. It remained, limp and lifeless, across Gary's shoulder. The arm wasn't a part of him anymore.

Skip panicked. *I can't move. I'm going to die. I'll never play football again,* he thought.

He began to sense pain. He had been numb all over, but now he felt as if someone were pushing hundreds of pins into his body. Then he felt a burning sensation. Both feelings started in his feet and he could feel them—the pins, the burning—moving up, until he felt the pain over every inch of his body.

Skip didn't try to talk. He tried only to keep his eyes open so that he could see Gary, who continued to lean over him. Gary was his only link with what was real and what was alive. Skip desperately wanted to hold onto that.

"OK, fella. Take it easy. You're going to be all right." The voice was unfamiliar.

Skip looked up. A man in a white uniform was bending over him. Skip tried to smile at him; he was too weak now to try to talk.

The attendant and his partners eased a wire-mesh stretcher under Skip, using the buoyance of the water to lift his limp body gently. They lifted the basket out of the water, careful to keep it level, and carried him to the ambulance. The attendant never left his side, holding Skip's head straight throughout the ten-minute ride to the hospital.

The two men carried him into the emergency entrance of General Hospital of Virginia Beach and put him on an examining table.

Skip asked what was wrong. The answer was noncommittal.

A doctor began to work on Skip. He asked Skip to tell him when there was feeling. Skip waited for the doctor to start. Then he realized that the doctor was already moving along his body, probing with some kind of instrument. He wanted to feel something, to be able to tell the doctor that the probe hurt. He talked to himself, urging his mind to recognize pain, pressure, anything, just so he could tell the doctor.

"Yeah, I can feel it," Skip muttered. The doctor had worked his way from Skip's feet up to his chest. Skip had felt the instrument's prick near his breastbone. That was all that he had felt. He was relieved at sensing pain, but he was frightened that he had not felt the other jabs. The doctor was holding a large pin.

The doctor lifted Skip's right arm and began slowly to move the fingers back and forth. Skip looked at the arm. He felt nothing. It was as if it weren't attached to his body. The doctor moved around the table and repeated the exercise with Skip's left arm. Again, Skip felt nothing. He wanted to stand up. He knew everything would be all right if he could just stand up.

The doctor moved away.

Skip was alone in the examining cubicle. He tried to remember what had happened, why he was in the hospital, where Gary and the girls were. The answers wouldn't come. He was on the verge of crying, but he was too scared. A high school graduate. On his way to college with a football scholarship. He wanted someone to tell him that he was going to be all right.

2

The Very Worst

It had begun as a very ordinary day. Patsy Wilkins and her two young daughters, Karen and Shirley, were having lunch in the drugstore of the shopping center where Skip was working. He had come in for Cokes and coffee for his fellow workers. She had told him to be careful that afternoon at Lake Joyce. He had smiled at her and responded as he always did when she was protective, "Aw, Mom, come on." Then he left.

Later that afternoon at home, the phone rang. It was Yvonne O'Brien, the mother of Skip's friend, Gary.

"Patsy," Yvonne said, "Gary just called. There's been an accident with the boat. Skip's been hurt. He's at Virginia Beach Hospital now. You need to go."

"Yvonne, he's not cut up, is he?" The ugliness of propellers slicing into Skip's body flashed through her mind.

"No. No, Patsy, he's not cut up."

"Are you sure? 'Cause I'd have to call Tommy. I don't think I could handle that."

"No, he's not cut," Yvonne reassured her. "He's all right, really, just shaken up, I think. But I think you'd better come on down."

Patsy pressed the disconnect button on the phone and dialed the house where her oldest daughter, Linda, was babysitting.

"Linda. It's Mom. Skip's been hurt. I have to go to the hospital. But I need to send the girls over to you."

Linda's voice was calm. "OK. Now everything's going to be all right. Don't get upset. And be careful driving. He's fine, I'm sure."

Patsy directed Karen and Shirley to the neighbor's house and set out for the hospital, talking to herself the whole way, reminding herself to stay calm.

When she pulled up to the emergency room entrance, she spotted Gary O'Brien sitting outside, crying. Patsy stooped down and put her hands on his shoulders. "Gary," she said, "there's nothing to cry about. You know Skippy's going to be fine."

As soon as Patsy identified herself to the nurse at the counter, she was ushered into the emergency area where starched white curtains were pulled back at the front of each small cubicle. A doctor met her.

"Mrs. Wilkins, your son is resting comfortably right now. But he's injured his neck. Badly. It may be broken."

Patsy nodded to the doctor and headed toward the one cubicle that was occupied. Nearing the foot of the bed, she recognized her son. He was lying still. Only his chest moved, heaving slightly with his breathing. His arms were folded across his chest, his eyes were closed. What she could see of his shoulders above the sheet was deeply tanned from weekends of surfing and being on the beach. There were no marks, no wounds on her son. She went limp with relief.

Skip opened his eyes. He didn't know how long he had been lying there, alone. It had seemed like forever. *The ugly nightmare,* he thought, *must be over.* His mom stood next to him.

"Skippy, don't you worry. You're going to be fine. God will take care of you. You know that."

She leaned down and gently kissed his cheek. Skip felt a tear form in the corner of his eye and roll down the side of his face.

"I hope so, Mom," Skip said in a weak voice. "I sure hope so."

Patsy composed herself before she dialed her husband's number at work.

The phone rang in Tommy Wilkins' office shortly after lunch. His wife's voice was controlled, her message concise.

"Tommy . . . Tommy, I think you'd better leave work if you can. Skippy's been hurt. Honey, I think he's hurt real bad. It's a neck injury, they say. Please hurry. He's at Virginia Beach General. In the emergency room."

"I'll leave right now," Tommy said.

When Patsy Wilkins hung up the phone a doctor appeared at her side and motioned her toward the semi-privacy of the emergency room, away from the corridor.

"Mrs. Wilkins," he said, "we're going to have to transfer your son to Norfolk General."

"Why?" Patsy asked. "Isn't he all right here? He looks fine. What is—"

The doctor broke in. His voice was soft, but urgent.

"Mrs. Wilkins, it does appear that your son has a broken neck. We don't have a neurosurgeon here."

"No. No, wait a minute." Patsy panicked. "I have to call my husband. Skippy's uncle is a doctor and I want to talk to him. He'll know what to do."

This time the doctor let her finish. Then he spoke. "Mrs. Wilkins, we've just contacted Norfolk General. They are expecting him. And we've talked to the doctors there and they'll be waiting. You can ride with your son, but we really do need to move him as quickly as we can."

Patsy rushed back to the phone. She dialed Tommy's number again to tell him to go to Norfolk General. She was told that he had already left the office. She was frantic, but only for a moment. Skip was being rolled out of the emergency room and toward the door.

Two men in the white uniforms of the volunteer rescue squad carefully collapsed and locked the legs of the stretcher-bed and lifted it and its occupant into the back of the ambulance.

Patsy and an attendant sat in the back with Skip.

The ride was uneventful for the first ten minutes and Patsy began to relax, although she didn't take her eyes off her son's face.

Then Skip began to vomit. A watery green liquid oozed out of the side of his mouth and ran down his cheek. Before the attendant could move to him, his body began contracting as the lake water and weed particles in his system were regurgitated in waves of green. He began to choke. He gasped for air. He couldn't breathe.

Patsy wanted to scream and get out of the ambulance. But she couldn't take her eyes off her son.

The attendant reached behind Skip's head and neck with both hands, quickly and carefully turning Skip's head ever so slightly to allow him to empty his mouth and throat and begin to breathe. All the while the attendant talked to him and reassured him.

The attendant leaned toward the small window to the cab and driver. In a soft and matter-of-fact voice, he said, "He's going into shock. He's into shock, I think."

The attendant worked to keep Skip's throat clear. When the vomiting appeared to end, he cleaned Skip's face and placed an oxygen mask over Skip's mouth and nose.

As soon as the ambulance pulled in front of the emergency room doors, attendants came out and assisted in getting Skip inside.

A doctor told Patsy that they were going to take X rays and that she should try not to worry, that they would get back to her as soon as they knew something.

As the doctors began their examination, Patsy found herself once again trying to deal with the events of the past two hours. She prayed and talked to God. It helped, but she knew she would feel better when her husband came. She wondered how long it would take. He'd have to go to the Beach hospital first, then retrace part of his journey back into Norfolk. *Hurry. Please hurry, Tommy. I can't hold on much longer,* she thought.

Tommy Wilkins was halfway along the twenty-mile drive to the Beach when an ambulance passed him heading toward Norfolk. He wondered who was inside. Was it Skip? Would they move him? Would Patsy have found the time to call?

He drove on, knowing only the words of Patsy's message. Emergency room. Virginia Beach. Tommy arrived and told the emergency room nurse who he was.

"I'm sorry, Mr. Wilkins. Your son was transferred to Norfolk General," she said. "They left about an hour ago."

Tommy returned to the car and to the highway he had just traveled. It would be a long way back. His mind kept ticking through the endless possibilities of what he might find at the hospital.

The parking lot outside Norfolk General's emergency room was full. Tommy pulled his car to a halt in a "No Parking" zone. Fear and the queasiness in his stomach were rising. He thought he was going to be sick when he saw the sign, "Emergency Room Entrance." As he rushed through the hospital doors, his mouth was dry, and his heart was pounding.

But just the sight of her husband relieved Patsy. Suddenly she believed that everything would be all right. Quickly she told Tommy what she knew, and he disappeared into the emergency room cubicle that held his son.

Tommy Wilkins looked down at his son lying on the examining table. A soiled, wet sheet covered Skip's body up to his neck.

He clenched his teeth and called up all of his strength and self-control. He reached down, clasped his hand over his son's hand, and looked into terrified eyes.

"Skip . . . son . . . you've got . . . you've got a broken neck."

Tommy battled against the emotions trying to take control. He raged inside at what he had been told, at the words he had just spoken to his son. But he wouldn't crumble. He wouldn't yield. He would battle from this moment to see his son well and whole again. He would never quit. Above all, he would never let his son know how much pain would come with the sentence he had just spoken. He wanted desperately to throw himself on his son's helpless body, but he maintained his composure and squeezed hard on Skip's hand.

"I have to go now. For a while. But your Uncle Bill will be with you. And your mom and I will be with you in a little while."

Tommy retreated slowly from Skip's side. He took a deep breath and walked softly out of the small, orderly examining cubicle. He let the tears come.

Shortly after his father's visit, Skip was moved from the emergency room into the operating room. He was aware of the change because the bright lights that had made his eyes tired were replaced by softer yellow lights. The voices and the noises were clearer for longer periods of time.

He heard his Uncle Bill's voice.

"Skip, this is Dr. Neal. He's going to help you. Can you listen to him for a minute?" William E. Butler, sixty-five, a general surgeon and Tommy Wilkins' uncle, slowly moved out of Skip's view. In his place was another man. He was a young, short man with glasses, who stuttered ever so slightly.

The man bent over Skip.

"Skip, I'm Dr. Neal. We're going to have to do a few things to you to straighten your neck. They won't hurt. But I want to tell you what we're going to do."

Skip murmured, indicating that he was listening.

"We're going to put some things in your head to hold your neck straight. We'll have to shave your head. You'll feel a prick perhaps. And you'll hear the sound of a drill. It won't hurt. I want you to just relax as much as you can."

Skip murmured again.

Richard K. Neal, Jr., a young Norfolk neurosurgeon who was rapidly gaining an excellent reputation, was now behind Skip's head. There was movement, but Skip couldn't see. Then he felt a slight tugging sensation at his scalp.

The doctor carefully clipped away the sun-bleached hair. Then he lathered the remaining close-cropped hair with soap and began to shave Skip's head. Skip felt pulls at his scalp. Then he felt waves of pain as the razor was scraped over and over against his scalp, removing any trace of hair. In spite of the pain, Skip tried to visualize what he would look like with no hair.

Dumb, he thought to himself.

Dr. Neal leaned over him again.

"Skip, you're going to feel a slight pinch on the right side of your head. It won't last but a second," he said softly.

Skip did feel the pinch. It didn't hurt, just as Dr. Neal had said.

After a short silence, Skip thought he heard the whine of a drill. He felt a slight pressure against his head. Then he was sure he heard the sound of a drill. It was close to him, just above his right ear.

The sound stopped.

Then he heard it again, this time close to his left ear. He again felt slight pressure against his skull, but no pain.

Skip was tired. Very tired. He couldn't fully accept the fact that he was lying on a hospital table. He blinked to stay awake.

There was a different sound now. The drilling noise had stopped. Skip could hear, very clearly, a slow crunching sound.

The noise continued. Then stopped.

It started again. Then stopped again.

There was a rhythm to it. A pattern. Someone was turning a screw.

The sound stopped again. After a longer time it began again. Skip recognized the same rhythm.

He was horrified. They were screwing something into his head! He wanted to scream, to leap off the table, to get out, but his arms and legs wouldn't move. He was a captive inside his body.

The crunching sound stopped and Dr. Neal looked down at Skip again.

"We're all finished for right now, Skip. You've done just fine. I'll be back in a few minutes. I want to talk to your mother and father," he said.

The quiet that briefly enveloped Skip was broken by the voice of a black man in a white uniform.

"I'm gonna have to cut your bathing suit off you. Won't hurt. You just relax," the orderly said.

Skip thought about the suit. A Hang-Ten. Almost new. *No,* he thought. *Why would he want to cut it?*

He managed to speak. "No. It's a new Hang-Ten. You can't cut it. I'll need it later."

The man retreated, pulling the curtain open, then closing it. Skip was beginning to hate the sound of the metal rings sliding across the curtain rod. The sound meant either someone was coming to do something to his body, or someone was leaving him alone with his fear and confusion.

Skip heard the man talking to a nurse outside the curtain.

"He doesn't want it cut off him. What should I do?" the man asked the nurse.

"I'll see what I can do," she replied.

Then the sound of the curtain opening and closing again.

The nurse smiled down at Skip. "We have to get it off. But maybe we don't have to cut it. Let's try," she said.

The nurse and the orderly worked slowly and carefully, easing the suit down and finally off. Skip felt nothing as the two of them moved his legs to remove the suit.

A new doctor came in.

"Skip. Skip, you're doing just fine. We're going to catheterize you now. And then we'll let you get some rest," he said.

The doctor continued, anticipating the question asked by Skip's puzzled and frightened look.

"Skip, you're paralyzed. You can't void. This will help you," he said.

Skip was still confused. He still didn't know what was going to happen. But he didn't ask.

The doctor continued to explain.

"It's a small tube. We are going to insert it into your penis. You won't feel it. I promise you."

Skip surrendered completely to mounting terror. The shaving. The drill. The sound of the screws. Now they were going to put something inside his penis.

He had, until that moment, tried to find the courage and the strength to ask one more question. Now he was too scared to ask whether he was going to die.

Patsy and Tommy rose from their chairs in the waiting area of the emergency room when they saw Bill Butler coming toward them.

Tears trickled down his face as he joined them. He was a doctor. But he was also family. And the family part of him ruled now.

He looked first at Tommy, then at Patsy. He blinked his eyes, then spoke to them.

"You know, I only wish that it were me in there."

"Uncle Bill. Oh, Uncle Bill. Why do you say that?" Patsy asked.

"Because my life is almost over. And his is just beginning. He has so much promise."

He paused a moment. "Patsy, Skip may never walk again." His voice cracked as the words came out.

"You need to talk to Dr. Neal. But I thought I ought to tell you that myself."

Dr. Neal joined them.

He recognized the question in their minds by the fright in their eyes. He waited a second to see if they wanted to speak. When they didn't, he gave them the only answer he had.

"It is very, very bad. The very worst. He will probably never walk again."

"No," Patsy said firmly. "He'll walk again. He will walk. Skippy will walk."

Dr. Neal touched her arm.

"You hang on to that faith," he said.

Dr. Neal told them that Skip was being moved to an operating room and then would be put in the intensive care unit. He suggested that they would be more comfortable in the family waiting room on the ICU ward. Then he returned to Skip.

When the elevator doors opened on to the ICU floor, Patsy and Tommy saw dozens of people already in the halls and crowding the main waiting room. Friends. Family. Boys who they recognized as Skip's friends.

The knots of people clogging the hallway parted as Tommy and Patsy made their way to the family waiting room. Hands reached out to pat them, heads nodded to them, but no one spoke because no one knew what to say.

The word had spread rapidly about Skip—from Linda to Skip's grandparents, from Gary to Skip's friends. Adults and high school students had stopped what they were doing and driven to the hospital. Nobody really knew for sure what had happened, but all of them knew that it was serious. People continued to come in. Relatives and close family friends came into the family room to speak to Tommy and Patsy, then resumed their vigil in the hallway.

The waiting came to an end when Dr. Neal appeared.

"Before you go in and see him," he said, "I want you to understand what has happened." He explained that the fourth, fifth, and sixth vertebrae of Skip's spine had been crushed.

"Don't be alarmed when you see him. We've shaved his head in order to put him in Crutchfield tongs. They look a little bit like the tongs you'd use to lift a block of ice. They're to keep his neck in traction. He is conscious and you can talk to him for a minute."

Tommy and Patsy followed the doctor.

Neither of them had absorbed what Dr. Neal had told them. Neither of them knew what Crutchfield tongs were. They wanted only to see their son.

When Dr. Neal pulled back the curtain to the ICU cubicle, Tommy and Patsy Wilkins weren't prepared for the sight that was in front of them in the dim light.

Skip's body, naked to the waist, was fully developed and nearly perfect in its proportions. The well-defined muscles glistened from his tan even in the dimness. His was the body of a young athlete.

From his neck upwards, however, he was a picture of torture. He was bald. Dried blood splotched his forehead where his head had been scraped in the accident. Blood had dried around several cuts suffered when his head was shaved. Tongs, large steel tongs, were clamped into his skull and attached to a cable running to the head of his bed. Blood that oozed from the drill holes had dried and crusted around the openings in his skull where the tip of the tongs entered. His head was fixed toward the ceiling, held immobile by the hideous tongs.

Patsy and Tommy Wilkins stood in a horror chamber. Their son was the victim. Each reached instinctively for the other's hand. When they touched, their hands fit together and each of them squeezed hard, trying to make the pain and awesomeness of what they saw go away.

They both moved to the head of the bed and leaned over so that Skip could see them. Afraid to touch him, they continued to clasp hands.

Finally Patsy spoke. "Skippy. We're here. You're going to be fine now. The doctors are taking care of you. And God is going to look after you. You hear?"

Tommy leaned close to his son. "Skip, we're going to be with you. We're going to work this out. You're going to be all right, son."

Skip's eyes acknowledged that he heard their words.

They stepped back from the bed and slowly walked out of the room back to the waiting room.

Dr. Neal joined them. "If you are praying people, now is the time to pray." He squeezed each of them on the arm and returned to ICU.

Patsy sat on the sofa. She was quiet and calm for a moment. But then her mother, sitting next to her, began to sob. The vision of her son with the tongs in his head, lying so still on the bed, came back to Patsy. Tears flowed down her cheeks. She didn't try to stop them or wipe them away. She gazed at the wall straight ahead, crying.

Tommy had to walk. Anywhere. Down the hall. Anywhere. But he had to walk right now.

Friends nodded as he went past, but none spoke. They all saw his sadness.

When he reached the end of the hall, he came upon Paul Bradley, one of Skip's friends. As their eyes met, they both wept. They didn't speak, but somehow they both understood that Skip was in terrible trouble.

3

Why Harvey Shapiro Had Come

It was midnight when Patsy and Tommy Wilkins left the hospital and went home that first night. They slept for three hours, rising before dawn to return to the hospital where they waited for the precious five minutes out of each hour that they were allowed to be with their son.

The vigil that began the night before became a routine. Tommy and Patsy were constant occupants of the ICU waiting room. When they remembered to eat, they went to the hospital's snack bar. One or the other sometimes drove home for a while to help Linda with the two girls. But that was all they saw of the world outside Norfolk General during those first days.

The outside world, however, managed to intrude into their lives behind the hospital walls.

The local newspapers wanted to know about Skip: his accident, how it happened, his condition, his future. For the past two years, Skip's name, his picture, his athletic records in football and track, and his acceptance of a college football scholarship had been part of the local sports news. Now he was injured. The newspapers wanted to tell their readers how and how badly.

In addition, friends of the Wilkins family and Skip's school friends flooded the hospital switchboard with calls and questions.

The queries led to a discussion among the two Wilkins, the doctors, and the hospital administrator.

"We're going to have to release some kind of statement," the administrator said.

Tommy could see no problem. He and his wife were ready to acknowledge to the outside world exactly what they could understand: their son had a broken neck.

That phrase, however, was too blunt for the doctors and the administrator.

The statement, when released to the press, read that Skip "is progressing well. He has sustained severe neck injuries and is being treated in the intensive care unit of Norfolk General Hospital."

The news story told of the accident. It quoted Tommy as saying that his son had been skiing since he was six years old and that this was his first serious accident. But there was no reference in the story to Skip Wilkins' future. That question couldn't be answered yet.

As a result of his discussion with the doctors and the administrator about the newspaper statement, Tommy began to understand that he knew very little about Skip's condition. He realized that he needed to ask questions of every doctor and nurse assigned to his son. There were subtleties among medical people that he would never understand unless he began to question and question hard.

One thing that he and Patsy did understand, though, was the ever-present possibility of death during the first days of Skip's hospitalization.

Dr. Neal had explained to them that swelling could set in as a result of the crushed vertebrae. The swelling, throughout Skip's body, would begin slowly and unhaltingly to squeeze off his air supply. This shock to his already weakened system would be followed by death.

If the swelling started—and it was most likely to occur during the first seventy-two hours after the accident—there was little that anyone could do to reverse the outcome.

Each time Patsy and Tommy saw Dr. Neal during the first days and nights, their immediate comfort in his presence gave way to fear when he started to speak. But each time, Dr. Neal reported,

"He's holding his own." Relief would give them more courage for the next meeting.

They tried not to think about what could happen, but it was there. Minute after waking minute, they lived with the knowledge that their son could begin to die.

Early on the morning of the fourth day, Dr. Neal had a different message. "He's made it. He's passed this crisis. I don't think that we need to worry about the swelling anymore. I think it would have begun before now. We've been very fortunate." He smiled at them. He still had a lot to do for his young patient, but he was aware that his words gave new strength and hope to the Wilkinses.

Tommy and Patsy grabbed at the news, viewing it as a major victory. They wanted to know what the next step would be.

"If he continues to show improvement," Dr. Neal said, "the next move will be out of ICU and into a regular room. He's a remarkable young man. Without his strength and physical conditioning, I don't think he would have come this far. I know it's hard to see right now, but you are fortunate that he is such a strong young man."

A move out of ICU became the next prayed-for event in the life of the Wilkins family.

Tommy, without knowing why and without telling anyone, began to keep a diary on Skip in a small pocket-size notebook that he had pulled from his sportcoat the first night in the hospital.

His first entry began:

6-12-67 Injured . . . Doctor's comment: The future looks very dim.

On June 19, the eighth day of Skip's stay in ICU, Tommy turned slowly through the notebook as he waited for the time he could see his son.

There had been little to note during the previous days. Mostly, the entries read: "Pain and uncomfortable." or "Soft diet. Liquids." The last two days the notation in the small book had read simply: "Sick stomach."

Tommy wondered what this eighth day and night would bring to his son.

Skip seemed stronger and more rested when Tommy and Patsy reached the side of his bed. His stomach was settled and he had been able to hold down some liquids.

There had been little conversation among the three during the past days and nights. Skip either had been in pain or exhausted. Now he wanted to talk.

"You know how you two have been telling me that God will take care of me, Mom? And Dad, you told me that God will show us the purpose in all of this. Well, I've been thinking . . ." Skip paused.

He took a deep breath and continued.

"Well, I've made up my mind that I am going to get better. I know that God will take care of me. And if he does, I'm going to be in college in the fall. I won't be able to play football, I know. Not this year. But I'll be strong enough to play next year. And if I work hard enough, I can play pro ball after college. I'm going to do it. I've decided. I'm going to do it as a testimony to God."

His parents didn't try to discourage him; they had witnessed the first positive sign from their son. There would be time enough later to tell Skip the truth about his condition, when he was stronger and could handle it. They let him continue to talk, easing his mind by agreeing with him that the coach at Elon College would probably hold his scholarship open until next season.

As Tommy sat again in the waiting room urging the clock to speed its hands so he could be with his son one more time, he reached for his notebook. Under the date of June 19, 1967, he wrote:

Skip said college next year. No football. Then good at football and pro ball as a testimony to God!

Tommy Wilkins wanted to believe that it could be done, but he knew better. He had seen the X rays. Perhaps someday there would be football, but it wouldn't be next year.

Skip, lying quietly in bed, thought about his decision. Since he was a child, he had never doubted God's existence. He'd been raised to believe. Now, with God as his only hope, he was more than willing to promise that his recovery and a football career would be a testimony to the God that his mother and his father kept so close to them.

Time began to be measured in victories and defeats, not days and nights. Hope and despair traveled sometimes on the smallest of events.

Skip's only body movement was with his right arm. Frequently he would sense his nose itching. Or the set of prism glasses that allowed him some outward vision began to cause headaches. On those occasions, he would instinctively raise his arm toward his face. With concentration, he could lift it into the air. The muscles remained in deep shock. When his arm neared a vertical position, it became uncontrollable and fell back as dead weight, frequently smashing down across his face.

He developed serious nose bleeds as his wrist constantly slammed down against his nose. Finally a doctor was summoned to pack his nose. Skip told him that he felt like something was caught in his throat. He couldn't breath well. The doctor suctioned his throat, clearing the passage of blood that had been continually collecting from his damaged nose.

Skip spent a restless night and had increasing difficulty in taking deep breaths. When the nurse came in for morning rounds, Skip told her that he thought he had something in his throat. First one nurse, then a second examined him. They saw nothing.

Uncle Bill appeared at his bedside as he had done each morning since Skip had been admitted. It was one way that Skip could tell when morning came in the dim, unchanging world of ICU.

"How're you feeling this morning, Skip? Sleep well last night?" he asked his nephew.

"I can't breathe, Uncle Bill. I feel like something's in my throat."

Bill Butler examined his throat.

He became urgent, demanding a spittle. He reached his hand into Skip's mouth, searching the throat with his fingers.

Skip gagged. He thought he was going to vomit. It felt as though his uncle's whole fist was in his throat. Skip felt a sucking sensation, then the sensation of an object moving in his throat. His mouth filled up.

His uncle withdrew his hand and carefully turned Skip's head to one side. Instinctively Skip discharged the contents of his mouth. A large blood clot fell into the spittle.

"This boy could have choked to death," he heard his uncle tell the nurses.

"The next time he says he has something in his throat, there *is* something in his throat. Either get it out yourselves or call a doctor. Let's get a humidifier in here. That will help his breathing."

The following day brought a victory. Skip was moved from ICU to the C Wing of Norfolk General. Almost daily Tommy or Patsy had asked Dr. Neal when Skip could be moved; it became an obsession with them. Dr. Neal had seen some improvement in his patient, and he believed that the more time Skip's parents could spend with him, the more quickly Skip might regain his spirits and his strength. Dr. Neal now felt that a move from ICU was medically and emotionally wise. Elation showed on Skip's face and on Patsy's as she walked beside her son, while attendants wheeled him down the corridors to a hospital room.

The move, when it was completed, was not joyous. C Wing was in the older section of the hospital. New paint would have been welcome and the room was not bright and airy. An older man, who had suffered a broken neck, was in one of the two beds. A woman and a child were visiting in the room when Skip was wheeled in. The patient was smoking. A television set was on, although no one seemed to be watching it.

Patsy was deflated. The atmosphere had been brighter and more pleasant in ICU. Skip, too, was hit by the sudden depressing change. The move had been built up in both of them as something positive. It wasn't. Patsy made up her mind that Skip would be moved, that day. When Tommy arrived from work, he quickly agreed. They tried to reach Dr. Neal. He was out of town. The nurses wouldn't move Skip without a doctor's authorization.

An unexpected visitor, however, took Skip's mind away from the depression of his surroundings—his football coach, John Grady. He had brought someone with him. The coach and Skip exchanged greetings.

"Skip, this is Johnny Cooke."

Skip looked up. Bending over him was a young man, tanned and athletic looking. He smiled down pleasantly at Skip.

"Hi, Skip. Glad to meet you. Coach Grady has told me about you. And about the accident.

"I've got something I want to tell you, something that happened to me not long ago."

Their eyes met for a moment.

"Skip, I broke my neck, too. It happened when I was in college."

Skip's eyes widened. The phrase again. Broken neck. This time the words were coming from a friend, someone Coach Grady had brought. And he was walking.

"You did?"

"Yeah, I sure did. And I had a thing on my head similar to yours. It was more like a chin strap with leather around the top. But it had a weight that held my head in place, just like yours."

"You're kidding. You couldn't have."

"I did. It was eighteen days before I could feel anything. Or even move my arm. Then I started to get some return. Now I'm fully recovered."

Skip looked at him. The visitor wasn't kidding. He was standing right there, beside the bed. No wheelchair. No crutches.

Standing. His words were the most encouraging words that Skip had heard.

The two men stayed for a brief time. As they said their good-byes, Skip looked at Johnny Cooke again.

If he got better in eighteen days, Skip thought to himself, *I'm going to be all right in eighteen days, too.* Eighteen days from the accident would be June 30. *That's the date,* Skip told himself, *that I'm going to get well.*

Skip had already been persuading himself that he would get well as soon as the tongs were removed. *After all,* he thought, *that's what is holding my head straight so my neck can heal.* He had another reason for wanting the tongs out. He had seen them in a mirror that his mother had held over him. The tongs made him look sick and ugly, and he knew that people didn't want to look at him with those things screwed into his head.

So now he had two goals. First, get the tongs out. Then get through the eighteen days.

Patsy's determination to have her son moved to another room was fueled further after Coach Grady and Johnny Cooke left. A class of student nurses came into the room. Their immediate lesson was the proper use of suppositories on paralysis patients, and Skip was to be the patient. Many of the nurses were no older than Skip. Patsy controlled her anger, but flatly told the senior nurse that Skip would not be used in such a lesson. She added that episode to her reasons to get him to a different room.

She was adamant about the move. She pulled a chair closer to Skip's bed and made herself comfortable. She had made up her mind that she was going to stay with her son until he was moved.

Visiting hours had been over for nearly an hour when a nurse came in. "Mrs. Wilkins, I'm afraid you'll have to leave now. We'll take good care of him until the morning."

"I'm not leaving, nurse, until he's out of this room," Patsy's voice was a near whisper because of the sleeping patients, but it conveyed determination.

The nurse withdrew and returned minutes later with the floor nurse.

"Mrs. Wilkins," the senior nurse said, "we do have to ask you to leave. Your son will be all right. We'll . . ."

Patsy cut her off.

"I'm not leaving. Not until he's moved. You can get anybody else you want to tell me to leave. But I'm not going. Period. Not until he's out of this wretched room."

The nurses retreated together. The next time one of them came into the room, nothing was said about leaving. Patsy had made her point.

During the night Skip was turned slightly to one side by the nurses. It was then he saw his fellow patient. The man's leg, lifeless from paralysis, was dangling out of the bedsheets at an awkward and painful-looking angle. The sight struck Skip with terror. The man suffered the same spinal damage as Skip. If the man had no feeling in his leg, then Skip couldn't feel anything in his own limb. He was looking at his own condition. For the first time, Skip acknowledged that he was paralyzed.

Visions of the past days rushed at him: the blips and beeps of the machines in ICU, the near darkness, the hushed tones of the nurses as they softly rolled a bed out of the room when a patient died. He saw his father leaning over him, telling him that his neck was broken. He felt the awful fear of dying after the doctor drilled into his head. Then came the blacking out from fright and exhaustion and waking in confusion. He had blotted from his mind all of the horror he had experienced then. Now the fear was once again overwhelming him.

He couldn't take his eyes off the leg dangling awkwardly from the bed next to him.

Patsy came to his bedside to check on him.

Only then was Skip able to force his eyes away from the reminder that he, too, was helpless and paralyzed. He looked up at his mother and pleaded softly.

"Mom, don't leave. Please don't leave me. I'm scared."

Patsy pulled the chair closer to his bed for the night.

The next morning Patsy and Tommy continued their pressure to have Skip moved. They had a discussion with Dr. Neal, who had come back on duty. He did not feel that Skip had to be moved.

"I don't care. I want him moved. Out of this room," Patsy interrupted, her voice trembling with anger.

Dr. Neal needed these two people on his side. Skip's battle was going to be tough enough without a feud between his parents and his doctor over a room. Dr. Neal deferred and Skip was moved. A sense of victory returned to Skip and his parents. He was out of ICU and was going into better surroundings, Room 647 in the A Wing.

Within hours of his transfer, baskets of fruit began to arrive. The next day several cards came in the mail. The grapevine was at work again. His relatives, advised of the transfer out of ICU, passed the information to Skip's friends. A recreation center close to Skip's home raised enough money to buy him a television set.

Skip's spirits began to climb, but most of his body remained limp and lifeless. His chart, had he been allowed to see it, would have sucked out his remaining strength and fight. "Quadriplegia below the C-6 dermatomal level. He has anesthesia below the C-6 level. . . . The function of his tricep muscles, finger flexors, intrinsic hand muscles, intercostal and legs is absent."

There were days when the medical staff thought there might be some response in his legs, only to find a day later that it had disappeared. Tommy recorded each incident in his notebook, his own spirits rising and falling with the content of each cryptic phrase.

Twelve days after the accident, Skip managed another victory. His stomach had rebelled at almost every solid that he had been fed. His relatives brought all kinds of food to him, hoping to discover something that his system would not reject. One afternoon his uncle, Eddie Hutcheson, brought a handful of grapes and tentatively fed them to his nephew. Skip enjoyed them and they stayed down. Shortly after that discovery, Tommy began to place a single grape in his open palm and encourage Skip to try to pick it up and eat it. The exercise was agonizing. Skip had so little use of his fingers that he was unable to hold a grape, but he kept trying. Hour upon hour and day following day of patience and effort finally brought results. He was able to grasp a grape between the knuckle of his thumb and his index finger without crushing or dropping it.

He had lost so much ability in his arm that the limb would still collapse when he lifted it into the air. His hand, still holding the grape, would fall across his face, sometimes reinjuring his nose, other times bruising his mouth or chin. It was on a Saturday, as Tommy held the grape in his hand and encouraged his son to pick it up, that Skip managed to get a single grape into his mouth.

He had fed himself.

It was a single grape, but it also was another sign of progress for father and son. That night Tommy entered the feat in his well-thumbed notebook.

There was no sign of the use of muscles or nerves returning, however. The doctors and nurses rotated the checks they made over his body. One day they worked with his fingers, the next his arms, then his legs. Occasionally there was a sudden movement in a limb. Once both legs appeared to respond to a stimulus in one leg. But the doctors patiently explained away Tommy's hope for his son's recovery. They explained that muscle spasms occurred, even in cases of paralysis.

Skip was aware only that he was making progress. He didn't ask for details. He didn't want to know anything except when he would get well. So he didn't ask. And neither his parents nor his doctors volunteered anything except encouragement and frequent compliments about his cooperation with the ceaseless picking and probing at his body.

He found increasing comfort and enjoyment in the stream of friends and acquaintances who came to visit. Each person's appearance at the door to his room brought a genuine smile to his face. Some were timid in coming into the room; some were awkward in trying to find something to say, but Skip was relaxed with all of his visitors and they quickly relaxed in his presence. He kidded with his friends and joked about his appearance. He was losing weight, his suntan had faded, and his hair, beginning to grow out again, was too long to lie flat and too short to respond to a comb or brush.

He felt a sense of obligation to everyone who expressed concern about him. Almost daily, there was some new acknowledgement of his courage. Local radio stations periodically mentioned him and asked listeners to send cards and offer prayers of recovery for him. A group of friends organized a benefit dance to raise funds for his family. His entire recreation league softball team, all in uniform, came to see him before one of their games.

One day Harvey Shapiro called and wanted to come by to visit. Skip was puzzled. Why would Harvey come by? They had gone to junior high together, but Harvey had been injured in a diving accident in the ninth grade and Skip had seen him only once since then—sitting in a wheelchair at a party.

As Skip still pondered the question, there was a knock on the door.

In a moment, the smiling face of Harvey Shapiro was in Skip's full view. Skip remembered now that Harvey had been small. He hadn't grown in the three years since junior high. He seemed even smaller now, swallowed up in his wheelchair. Harvey's father spoke to Skip and took a seat by the window.

As the two boys chatted about the few mutual friends that they still shared, Skip began to wonder how Harvey had dealt with his accident. Living in a wheelchair. *How,* Skip wondered, *can Harvey smile and laugh and seem so content after all he's been through and what he has to look forward to? Three years in a wheelchair and he'll probably never get out of it.*

Harvey began telling Skip of his experiences. Soon Skip was hearing some of the same words and terms that he heard from his own doctors.

As Harvey talked, he spoke of people's reactions to a crippled individual, how his mind wasn't crippled and how some people were able to accept him as a person in spite of the wheelchair. He told Skip about his ability to go places, with the help of the attendant his family had found. He said that he was able to have fun with other young people, even drink and go to parties.

The longer Harvey talked, the more Skip wished that he would go away. Skip knew that he was different. He was going to get well. Johnny Cooke had gotten well, hadn't he?

Harvey and his father finally left. Skip was relieved, but the things that Harvey had told him stuck in his mind. He tried to tell himself that he was going to get well, just like Johnny Cooke. It was only days away. How many? He tried to do the mental arithmetic, but Harvey's story kept getting in the way.

Finally Skip thought he understood why Harvey Shapiro had come to see him. He had come to help, to tell Skip what lay ahead, to help him realize that he was in for disappointments, but that life for a cripple wasn't all bad.

Skip tried to reject the possibility, but the vision of Johnny Cooke standing tall and straight and healthy beside his bed kept fading away. In its place was the picture of Harvey Shapiro in a wheelchair.

It was the last time that Skip would put all of his hope in Johnny Cooke's visit and it was the last time that he would secretly count the days—the eighteen magic days—until he got well.

Somewhere between what had happened to Johnny Cooke and what was never going to happen to Harvey Shapiro was the answer for Skip Wilkins.

Despite his growing apprehension about the future, Skip worked hard to be positive and cheerful with those around him, especially his parents.

There were times, though, especially at night when he was alone, that a sense of hopelessness would overcome him. In those moments, which he kept secret even from his parents, he always managed to rally, to look ahead, and to find hope by remembering the scores of people who cared about him and who kept him in their thoughts and prayers.

Skip's improving spirits and his interest in his visitors provided an opportunity for Tommy and Patsy to survey their worlds outside the hospital's walls and to turn their attentions for a while to their other responsibilities.

Tommy began to concentrate on his job with renewed dedication. He had stayed at the hospital for nine days and there was plenty of work to be caught up. When he returned to the office, his boss called for him.

"Tommy," he said, "I want you to know that we're all pulling for Skip. We know that he's going to make it through this thing all right. If we can help at all, just let us know. I know it's tough right now and I know that you want to be with him as much as you can. We'll work together with you. And if you have to be with him on short notice, just let us know."

This attitude at work, and the knowledge that he was highly regarded and that everyone was concerned about his son, kept Tommy going at his desk. In his own way, he felt a sense of obligation to the people who cared about him and his son.

Patsy found that she could slip away from Skip without worry when he was expecting visitors. She turned her attention to Linda, who had been managing the house and chores and taking care of Karen and Shirley.

Patsy was proud of her daughters. Since the afternoon when she had called her daughter to tell her that Skip had been hurt, Patsy had left the house and the two little girls to Linda's care. There had been no problems.

Linda, sixteen—two years younger than Skip—had admired her brother as long as she could remember. She had wanted to become a football player in grammar school because he was one. She had followed his athletics at every home game since his junior high years. They double-dated. She had never resented being "Skip's kid sister" although she had just ended an active year as a high school sophomore. She was worried about Skip, but she had found it natural to assume responsibility when her parents' lives suddenly were centered around hospital visits.

She drove her sisters every morning to Bible school, returned home and cleaned, picked up the girls, fixed lunches and suppers, and took them to playgrounds, to the beach, or to visit their friends. On some weekends, the three of them went to stay with Auntie and Uncle Ackie—Patsy's aunt, Irene Wagner, and her husband.

Linda managed to keep up her friendships with her schoolmates and she continued, when she could arrange it with her grandparents as chaperones, to have friends over to visit.

She had been raised as a member of a close and loving family. She was doing what was natural to her.

Only rarely did she overlook the things she knew her mother would want her to do. That was at mealtime. She and the girls loved pancakes. So pancakes were on almost every breakfast menu, just as hamburgers and french fries were served more than anything else at lunch and at supper.

Sometimes when she, her sisters, and their grandparents said prayers before bedtime, she would think of her brother lying in the hospital and feel tears in her tightly shut eyes. And though she would squeeze her eyes shut even harder, the tears still came.

Linda had a constant companion to help her around the house. Martha Chevalier was one of Linda's schoolmates and the girl whom Skip had been dating most often during the spring before school had ended. Martha had come to the house as soon as she heard about Skip's accident. From that first night, she was there whenever she could be. She helped Linda with the dishes and with the cleaning. She rode with her on the trips to Bible school. Sometimes she was there just to talk. Linda began to realize that Martha cared very deeply about Skip. And she wondered whether Skip knew that and whether he felt the same way.

Mike Whitley was always around to help the girls, too. He was a friend of both Linda and Skip. Without being asked, Mike took over all of the outdoor chores—cutting the grass, trimming the shrubs, and keeping the yard neat.

And sometimes in the background and sometimes in the center of things were Patsy's parents, Granny and Papa, and Auntie and Uncle Ackie. Whenever Linda and her sisters needed help, someone was there to lend a hand. Someone other than their parents, who couldn't be with them very often. Someone other than their brother, who couldn't be with them at all.

4

Not Left Behind

The date was June 30—eighteen days since Skip had been admitted to the hospital.

Dr. Neal asked Tommy and Patsy to meet him in the doctors' lounge. Tommy had learned that such a request meant a formal discussion about Skip. Perhaps some new development in his condition. Tommy was uneasy as he and Patsy walked toward the lounge.

"The time has come," Dr. Neal began as they sat down, "to make plans to move Skip."

Without waiting for their response, he continued.

"We have done nearly everything that we can do here. He's out of danger as far as shock and as far as further damage is concerned. But we can't do much more to help him gain further use of his remaining nerves and muscles. Assuming there is no unexpected setback, we should be able to remove the tongs in the next week or two. But Skip will need intensive rehabilitation and therapy. There are no facilities available in this area for that kind of treatment."

"OK. What do you recommend for him? And what should I begin to do?" Tommy was accustomed to his role as the questioner. From those first days he had started asking questions, writing down and remembering terms, learning degrees of physical disability by medical classifications. It had saved him from the feeling of being unable to help his son. He found most of the doctors and nurses helpful and understanding. But he began to realize that even they, with all of their knowledge and experience, did not always have absolute answers. In some cases, they had no answers that he and Patsy wanted to hear.

"There is a place in New York, Tommy. Rusk Institute. It's recognized as one of the leading rehabilitation clinics in the world for the kind of injury that Skip has. I am having my office gather together some information. I suggest that we begin now to try to get Skip in there very soon."

"Fine," Tommy said. "Just let me know what I need to do."

Patsy couldn't say anything. She was trying to sort out what she had just heard. She had never given any thought to Skip going anywhere except home.

Tommy sensed her attitude.

"Patsy, we don't have to worry. Skip's making progress, I know. But if Dr. Neal says that he needs to go to a special institute to get even better, then that's what we've got to do. No matter where he goes, we'll be able to see him and it'll be just that much sooner that he can come home for good."

Patsy nodded and tried to shake the feeling of separation that had already set in.

"I know," she said. "I know. It's just that I think he needs us to be with him. To make sure that he's taken care of."

"We'll always make sure of that. But we've got to do what the doctors think is best."

When Tommy arrived at the hospital the next day at lunch, he found his son groggy and tired. Skip had undergone routine and periodic kidney and blood tests. More X rays had been taken. Skip was complaining of a slight ache in his left shoulder, the side that had received the more severe damage. Dr. Neal had examined the shoulder several days earlier. Skip had been told that the slight pain he felt was normal.

Tommy began to act on the information that Dr. Neal's office had provided on Rusk Institute. He quickly hit an obstacle. He was told that Rusk had no available beds and that the institution could not take Skip for several months. He told Patsy, then counseled with Dr. Neal. The next best option was Woodrow Wilson Rehabilitation Center in Fisherville, Virginia. Patsy was relieved when she learned that it was only five hours from home. Tommy began his efforts anew.

Skip began to have frequent headaches. His shoulder remained sensitive. When Tommy visited one Friday morning, Skip complained of chills.

Tommy made a mental note to put an entry in his small diary later and began to help Skip eat some watermelon that had been brought to him. An hour later, the nurse brought lunch. Skip managed to down two bites, then he vomited. Tommy, sensitive to his son's every movement and every act, became convinced that something was going wrong.

Tommy's conviction turned into a reality. Skip began to run a low fever and his stomach rejected nearly everything. He began to lose his smile and his optimism. From time to time, he yielded to tears.

Dr. Neal ordered kidney tests for Skip. The tests revealed an infection, but Dr. Neal and a urologist he had called in were relieved. At least they knew where the problem was. Dr. Neal told Tommy and Patsy that at this point, it didn't appear to be too serious.

Skip was relieved, too, when Dr. Neal told him that it was a kidney infection. He had worried that something was going wrong with his spine and that he was going to suffer even more damage. His spirits were temporarily bolstered, too, when Dr. Neal told him that he was continuing to make progress.

Skip used the opportunity to urge that the tongs be taken out. Their removal remained an obsession with him.

"You're not quite ready for that, Skip. But it shouldn't be much longer. We'll see about them when I get back," Dr. Neal said. Later he left for several days off at nearby Nags Head, North Carolina.

The fact that Dr. Neal had told Skip that he would be going to some kind of rehabilitation place wasn't much consolation and didn't have much impact. It seemed too far away to grasp and, besides, nothing good was going to happen until the tongs came out. Skip believed that.

The medication prescribed for the kidney infection began to do its work quickly. Skip's fever continued, but his spirits improved and his smile came back.

"Good morning, Skip. How're you doing today?"

There was something extra in Dr. Thomson's usual morning greeting, Skip thought to himself. James L. Thomson had taken charge of Skip's case while Dr. Neal was away on vacation.

"Pretty good," Skip said. "Watcha gonna do to me today?"

"Oh, I don't know. Maybe something special. You've been a pretty good patient since Dr. Neal's been gone." Dr. Thomson was leaning over Skip, looking at his head.

Two nurses joined Dr. Thomson. The three of them, a nurse standing on each side of the bed, began working with the weight attached to the tongs. Skip could feel the movement, but he couldn't see what they were doing. He tried to detect what was happening from their soft and infrequent conversation, but he couldn't. He waited and wondered.

Dr. Thomson was again leaning over Skip's head.

Skip thought that the doctor was adjusting the tongs. Someone always seemed to be adjusting them.

Skip felt a slight pressure on one side of his head. He heard a small popping noise as his head was gently jerked to one side.

Suddenly Skip was frightened. He felt his head rolling from side to side. He tried to stop it, but it wouldn't obey.

"Try to relax, Skip. I know you feel funny. I've just taken the tongs out. They're gone for good."

Dr. Thomson's words didn't help. Skip's head still rolled from side to side. This wasn't the way it was supposed to be. He was supposed to be better when the tongs came out. But he wasn't. He was worse.

"Put them back," Skip pleaded. "Put them back. I'm going to hurt my neck again."

"OK, Skip. Just take it easy. Feels funny, I know. But you're fine. Doin' just fine. What you're experiencing is the lack of strong muscles in your neck. We've taken the tongs out and you don't have any support right now. Some of those muscles will come back pretty quickly and you'll be able to control your head. Don't you worry. I wouldn't let you out of here with your head wobbling all over the place. I have to think of my reputation."

Dr. Thomson grasped Skip's shoulder and squeezed it. He looked down at his patient with admiration. Skip managed to smile back.

Skip was exuberant when his parents arrived. He made no effort to suppress his happiness. To the three of them, but especially to Skip, the tongs had represented everything horrible about his injury. They were always there, an extension of his body, an ugly growth coming out of his head, a reminder that his injury was serious, so serious that doctors had to screw things into his skull and place tongs in his head.

The three were joyous. Tommy and Patsy kept asking Skip how it felt to be able to move his head; they kept telling him how well he looked, how normal and strong he appeared without the tongs. Skip, after the first confusing hour without the ability to control the movement of his head, now experienced the pleasure of being able to turn slowly from side to side and see items in the room that he had only been able to view through the prism glasses or when someone brought them within his narrow, and always upward, range of vision. The ability to turn his head was so basic, so simple. Yet, he had been deprived of that ability for thirty-eight days. Now he delighted in each slight turn, each new angle, and the ability to see in all directions.

Just as the dream of an eighteen-day recovery, like Johnny Cooke's, had faded against the reality of what doctors and medicine could and could not do, so did the healing power that Skip had conjured for the tongs. They were out now and he wasn't well. But he was better and that's what really mattered.

That night at home, Tommy got his notebook from his pocket. He printed in the largest handwriting that he had used to make his daily entries. The two words told of the biggest victory so far:

7-19-67 TONGS OUT!

The victory over the tongs was followed by a series of defeats. Skip's fever persisted and Dr. Neal was still out of town.

Tommy and Patsy became impatient with the treatment to reduce the fever. They pressured one of Dr. Neal's associates to do something more about the fever. He responded patiently that he was doing all that he could. Patsy remained concerned.

"With all he's been through, it would seem to me that you would be able at least to get rid of the fever," she told him.

The doctor leveled his eyes on hers.

"Look, Mrs. Wilkins. Your son's spinal cord has been destroyed. He will never walk again. You need to understand that. We will take care of the fever. But don't think for a minute that when the fever's gone your son is going to get up and walk out of here."

The words seared. No one, not even Dr. Neal, had said that Skip would *never* walk again. She knew the realization of that had stayed hidden deep in her mind. It had come to her on the first night when Dr. Neal had told them, "It is the worst, he may never walk again." But from that moment on, she had pushed that thought out of her consciousness. She wouldn't allow it. There wasn't room. Her thoughts were always on Skip's recovery, on the time when he would come home and start to live his life normally again. That night, for the first time, because of her harsh words about a fever, the thought that her son might never walk again returned to Patsy. This time she had to fight to force it out of her mind.

The fever broke and the kidney infection cleared up with a change in medication and in the type of voiding apparatus that Skip used.

As the kidneys began to clear, another complication developed. Skip's left thigh began to swell and redden. By this time Dr. Neal had returned, and his examination indicated a blood clot. He called in a specialist. Skip's leg was elevated and an Ace bandage was carefully wrapped around the thigh. He wasn't told how serious the situation was, but Tommy and Patsy were both cautioned to insure that great care was taken with the leg. If the clot moved into his lung, it could mean disaster.

The inflamed leg slowed Skip's introduction to a wheelchair. Several days after the tongs had been removed and he had been measured for a collar and a brace, attendants lifted Skip from his bed and placed him in a wheelchair. Within minutes he blacked out. The nurses had expected his reaction and caught him before he slumped and injured himself. Only the four-poster brace kept his head from nodding. He regained consciousness and tried to sit again. Within minutes, he vomited. His first lesson ended.

He became nauseated several more times before he was able to sit for twenty minutes, then thirty, then a full hour.

In bed, Skip wore a snugly fitting foam collar around his neck. The collar was replaced with the brace before he was lifted into the wheelchair for periods of sitting.

As Skip worked to build the strength needed to sit for longer and longer periods in a wheelchair, Tommy worked on the arrangements for Skip to go to Woodrow Wilson Rehabilitation Center.

After Dr. Neal's first mention of the center, Tommy had investigated it with the help of Leonard Strelitz, a longtime family friend. It was located two hundred miles away in the small town of Fishersville. The state had established it in 1947, converting a former Army hospital on the site into the nation's first state-owned and state-operated rehabilitation center.

Tommy had been told that the buildings in use were old, left over from the World War II years; but the state had started work on six new buildings. Two were already occupied. It had a good reputation, despite the age of the facilities. He'd been told by several doctors and some friends who had checked on the center that it offered some of the best rehabilitation services in the country for the severely handicapped.

He didn't much care about the looks of the place, as long as it offered some hope that his son could get additional help.

Skip's leg problem subsided and soon he was able to sit for long periods in a wheelchair. With the help of nurses and orderlies, he visited other patients in the hospital. Most of them knew from the hospital staff about Skip and his injury. He and his family had become favorites among the doctors, nurses, aides, and orderlies, many of whom frequented his room to chat or offer him an encouraging word.

On August 9, 1967, nearly two months after Skip had been admitted to Norfolk General Hospital, his father entered a message in his notebook. It read:

Good day. Maybe Woodrow Wilson next week.

For the next eight days, the small, informal diary of Tommy Wilkins read the same:

Good day.

Nurses from ICU, from the C Wing, and from the A Wing gathered outside the emergency room entrance. Orderlies formed another small congregation. Several doctors were present. All had been touched by Skip's determination. Dozens of other people, young and old, carefully dressed and casually dressed, milled outside the entrance. All friends of Skip, they had assembled to say good-bye.

Skip had no indication of the magnitude of the farewell as his stretcher was rolled outside the emergency room entrance.

When he appeared, the group of nurses, orderlies, friends, and relatives burst into spontaneous cheers and applause.

Tommy and Patsy, walking beside the stretcher, were taken aback, too. They had known that several of Skip's friends would be on hand to wish him good luck on his new journey. They hadn't expected members of the hospital staff.

It was a happy occasion for Skip. He managed to say only a couple of sentences before becoming emotional. He thanked the nurses, the orderlies, and the doctors for their care and for their interest in him. He thanked his friends for their concern and for their prayers.

Lastly, just before he was lifted into the ambulance, he thanked his parents and his family for everything that they had done. He acknowledged the sacrifices that they had made to be with him during his stay. He thanked Linda for her watchfulness over his younger sisters and for her care of the house. He wanted everyone to know how wonderful his family was.

Two rescue squadsmen gently lifted the stretcher and placed Skip in the ambulance. Patsy and Tommy climbed into the back with Skip and made themselves as comfortable as they could. His grandparents walked to their automobile. They planned to follow the ambulance.

As the crowd of people dominated by the white uniforms of nurses and orderlies waved and shouted their good-byes to Skip, the ambulance started slowly toward Fishersville, Virginia, and the Woodrow Wilson Rehabilitation Center.

Left behind in the warmth of the August sunshine were almost fifty people who had been touched by Skip's strength and his family's determination to see him well and whole again.

Left behind, as the ambulance pulled out of the driveway and turned onto the street, were hundreds of other people in Tidewater, Virginia, who had prayed for Skip's recovery and who would the next day be touched when they read in the newspapers that Skip Wilkins, high school athlete, had become strong enough to leave Norfolk General Hospital.

Not left behind on that warm August day were the memories, sometimes hazed by pain, fear, and lapses into unconsciousness, that Skip Wilkins alone possessed of his sixty-seven-day fight to stay alive.

5

One Part of Growing Up

As the ambulance maneuvered along the city streets to reach the highway leading to Fishersville, Skip's eyes were fixed on the scenes outside. Through the window across from his stretcher, just over his dad's shoulder, he caught glimpses of car tops, trucks and buses, storefront signs and buildings, and, once in a while, a person. He was out in the real world again. From the window in the hospital everything had seemed distant and remote, untouchable and unreal. Now he sensed the presence of other people and objects that he had once taken for granted. He savored the feeling of being alive.

As the ambulance reached the open highway and picked up speed, Skip shifted his gaze to his body, stretched down in front of him, covered by a sheet and a blanket. He took stock of his physique so often now that the sense of sadness and embarrassment was only momentary. He had lost one-third of his body weight during his hospitalization, and was down to 120 pounds. His chest, once thick and well-proportioned, was now only loose skin stretched across his rib cage. His arms were nearly bone thin. His biceps and triceps, developed during weeks and weeks of regimented exercise, had softened, then wasted away as he shed his weight.

The emaciated body, the gaunt face with deep-sunk eyes, the short, stubby hair was all that was left of the handsome, strong athlete of two months ago.

Skip shifted his gaze to his mom and dad, who were talking

quietly to each other. He studied them for a moment, then eased his head back to its normal straight position and closed his eyes. He thought about how much his parents had done for him during his life, how much love and care they had given to him and to his sisters, and how much patience they had needed to raise him.

With the swaying of the ambulance headed along the highway, Skip lapsed into a reverie.

His mind drifted to Currituck Sound in North Carolina where the family had bought a small lot. There he had learned how close and loving his family was. When he was eleven, they all shared the task of clearing the land for a trailer. Skip worked next to his dad, feeling the joy of working with his hands, of doing a job—any job—well, and realizing that work was a proper part of life. He came to love being on the Sound in the family's small, open runabout. More than anything, he liked to be alone in the boat. He would cruise slowly into the Sound, and as soon as he rounded the point and was out of sight, he would push the throttle wide open and experience the thrill of speed. Such trips always ended with his dad's shrill whistle, his index and little finger in each corner of his mouth, and the other hand above his head emphatically motioning for Skip to return to the landing. Once the boat was secured to the landing, he received a sharp-tongued lecture or restriction to the trailer, depending on how many times during that summer he had violated the rule against running the boat wide open. He was many years older before he understood how his father, on the shore, could tell when he, around the point and out of sight, opened the throttle. By then, his discovery of variable pitch was too late to prevent punishment.

He remembered the woods near his house. It had been his special place from the time that he was six years old. No punishment seemed strong enough to keep him in his own backyard. His dad had built a sandbox and swings, had cleared a large area for marble shooting, and later had put up a basketball backboard, but Skip still loved the freedom of the woods.

Maybe it was that love of freedom that got him into trouble in school and church. He thought of all the times he was ordered to the principal's office. At recess the energy that built up in him in class became a driving force as he darted around the playground, snatching hats or scarves from the girls and roughhousing with the boys.

It seemed to him that he had attended Sunday school and church with his parents as far back as he could remember. Sometimes he skipped Sunday school and went to the store near the church, buying candy with his offering money. Once in a while his teacher would discover his truancy and report it to his parents. Other times, after he had returned to the church grounds, the guilt would rise up and he would fear that God was going to punish him. Then, he would promise himself not to do it ever again. But the temptation the next time was greater than the recollection of his fright at God's possible wrath.

Skip's thoughts were interrupted by the slowing of the ambulance. It turned off the highway and came to a smooth stop.

"Skip," Tommy Wilkins said, "we're stopping here for gas. Do you want a Coke or anything?"

"Ah . . . a Coke," Skip answered.

His father smiled and patted Skip's shoulder as he stooped to make his way to the door.

Skip watched through the open door as Tommy headed toward the filling station, thinking about how much his dad had taught him through the years. When he was nine, they had worked together to close in the breezeway of their home to make a den. He remembered the tongue-lashings he'd receive when he'd daydream on the job and fail to respond to his father's instructions. His dad could become very angry, but somehow he always meted out the punishment in a way that left Skip still feeling wanted and loved.

Of all the people Skip knew and admired, his dad was the one person he wanted most of all never to disappoint. But there had been disappointments. The keenest ones, the ones that Skip most remembered, had come in athletics. It was there that father and son had a special bond and shared a special pride.

Skip's first athletic competition had come in the third grade, when he was selected to represent his class in a track meet. He took instantly to athletics, although he had to work hard at it.

In the seventh grade he had gained a starting position on the community league basketball team. He practiced longer and harder than the others, often working out with his dad in the backyard. By the last half of the season, he was the top scorer and the team leader.

But his dad cautioned him that athletics was only one part of growing up, that schoolwork was equally important. Although Skip always nodded his understanding after such talks, he couldn't find a way to enjoy homework and studying. Besides, his parents had always told him that they would be satisfied with Cs on his report cards.

As the end of basketball season approached, Skip turned all of his attention to the game. Twice his dad reminded him of poor grades and said that he had to improve his report card if he wanted to stay on the team. Skip heard the warning, but he didn't take it seriously. When his report card issued before the final two games of the season showed two Ds, he still didn't believe that his dad would halt his basketball play. But that night, after his dad got home and reviewed the grades, Skip was off the team. Skip had to call the coach and explain why he wouldn't be able to play. The embarrassment was almost as painful as the disappointment. When the phone call ended, Tommy Wilkins turned to Skip.

"Skip, I want you to know how disappointed I am in you. And for you. I wanted as much as you did for you to finish the season. Watching you play is a joy to me that you probably can't understand at your age. But your class work and your grades are the most important aspects of school. We haven't asked you to do something you can't do. We've asked only that you work and spend time with your studies. And you haven't done that. Now you pay the price."

It was the first time that Skip had approached a starring role; he couldn't understand how his father could deny him that. But it was denied.

The following year Skip tried out for the eighth grade football team. He was faster than his classmates, but smaller. He didn't make the team. His dad, however, helped him try out for the community league and he quickly learned the fundamentals and became a dependable running back.

He sat on the bench in eighth grade basketball for most of the season. That spring he failed to make a letter in track, yet he kept on trying.

His physique started to develop the summer before his ninth grade year. He landed a starting spot on the junior high school football team as an offensive end, but lost it before the season started to a transfer student. Still, Skip kept at the practice and the workouts at home, regaining his position and remaining in the starting lineup.

The next fall he was a sophomore at Princess Anne High School. The football season, however, was cut short for him by a broken ankle in the first game.

But Skip began to find himself athletically. Through the winter he ran indoor track, confident that he could make the spring varsity track team. He set his sights on his first varsity letter.

He remembered the excitement when he came home from school the afternoon that the members of the varsity team had been named. He ran up the steps, two at a time, and into his room. He sat on the bed for a moment, more out of breath from pure elation than from the race home. When he caught his breath, he stripped off his clothes, leaving them in a heap on the floor. Then, having donned the red and white varsity track uniform, he walked to the mirror.

He adjusted the red shorts and tucked the white shirt deeper into the pants. Turning sideways, he bent into the runner's starting-line stance. When he stood again, he smiled at his reflection and combed his sandy hair. For the first time in a long, long while, standing in front of the mirror, Skip Wilkins felt good. He'd made the team. A sophomore on the varsity track team.

The frustration and sense of failure from seasons past were gone. There was no room now in his thoughts for the broken ankle that had cut short the football season. No room for the fruitless hours he had spent on the basketball court only to watch the game from the bench.

Skip knew that he was going to be a track star.

He flopped back on the bed, stared at the ceiling, and thought back to the trial 440 that had won him the uniform. The day was rainy and only a few students and parents had shown up for the trials. No matter that the crowd was small. It seemed to him that the track's infield and stands were packed and that everyone was watching him, expecting him to stumble, to fall on his face.

He remembered the raw panic that set in as the starter raised the gun. And clearly, as though he were again running the race, he recalled the calm that overtook him as soon as he came out of the starting blocks. The practice—the lonely miles around the school track, the afternoon runs through the neighborhood—took over. His body functioned as a runner, an athlete. Even the pain—the shortness of breath and the ache in his lungs—was pleasurable. He had won; he liked first place.

He wondered briefly after that race whether Dave Grochmal was really as good as everyone at school said. And if he was so good, why hadn't Dave beaten him?

He looked at the clock on the dresser, rolled over and pushed himself up off the bed, and began to dress for supper. He looked in the mirror one more time before going downstairs.

Skip ran every practice as though it were a race. The first meet with rival Kellam High was all he could think about in class, on the track, at home in his room, during a lull at the dinner table. He kept telling himself that he would do well. Perhaps even win.

Finally, the day of the meet came. He couldn't remember ever being so nervous as he pawed at the track, getting settled into the starting blocks.

The gun sounded. He was out of the blocks ahead of the pack and in the lead. He was running hard and running well, coming into the first curve.

Then he heard it—feet behind him. Dave Grochmal passed him, running smoothly and effortlessly on his outside. Then a Kellam runner. And another Kellam runner.

He tried to make his legs churn faster. He shouted to them, "Faster!" Even before the third curve, his breath was coming hard, his arms and legs aching as he tried to pull up with the leaders. When he hit the back stretch, he knew he wouldn't catch anyone. But the disappointment didn't set in until he crossed the finish line. It was a huge wave sweeping over him. He was angry. Hot tears stung his eyes.

Dave Grochmal was beside him, an arm across his shoulder.

"Good try," he said, and moved on. Skip suddenly understood that what he had heard about Dave, the way Dave paced himself and timed his move, was true. Dave was good. Skip Wilkins had a way to go.

The next day at practice, Coach Sergeant moved Skip from the 440 to the 880. He had been watching him closely during the past weeks, and he explained that Skip might do better in a longer distance.

Skip didn't understand all of the reasons, but he saw the move as a new chance to prove himself. He began to do just that.

As Coach Sergeant had said, the 880 was Skip's race. He could maintain the same speed and pace as the 440. And he could keep it up the entire distance. Steady, even running, right up to the finish. He ran the 880 in the second meet and placed third.

He was part of the varsity now and he set his mind on winning races—and winning a letter.

A comfortable pattern developed. He was a member of the team. He ran the practice sprints all-out, winning them more often than not. It didn't matter that some of his teammates were loafing during practice; he still took pride in winning.

As the season progressed, Skip focused more and more on a varsity letter. He never shared his goal, not even with his dad. But he would think, often in class and always during practice, about the feeling he would have if he lettered as a sophomore.

The letter became the single most important aim in his life.

In early May, before the last two meets of the season, Coach Sergeant met with each member of the team to explain who had already made a letter and who still had a chance to earn one.

The letters were based on points earned during the season; three for an individual first place, two for a second, and one for third place. The members of the relay teams had to divide the points the team earned.

Skip needed only two points to letter. If he placed at least third in each of the last two meets, he could do it.

Norfolk's Maury High meet was the tougher of the two. The team had two of the best 880 runners in the state. Skip came in third in that race, crossing the line just behind them.

He was confident of a letter now. His attitude was positive, he had long since become a true member of the team, and he knew how to pace himself, how to train, and how to win.

The night of the city meet, the stands and the infield were jammed with parents and students from all the Virginia Beach high schools.

Skip took some easy laps on the inside of the track as the time for the 880 got nearer.

He had never seen so many people. The guns going off for the sprints and the other runners in their school colors added to the excitement.

Then he was listening to Coach Sergeant:

"Skip, Don Rhodes pulled a muscle in the 440. I've got to pull you from the 880. I want you to run the second leg of the relay."

Skip was heartsick. He had run the relay several times during the season, but it wasn't his event. He thought about the letter and he started to ask the coach what the change would mean. But Sergeant was gone.

Skip had to know about the letter. He ran after the coach and caught up with him.

"What about a letter?" he blurted.

He remembered only that Sergeant had said, "If we win the relay, you'll letter."

He tried to grab hold of the enthusiasm that always came with the members of the relay team. But it didn't come. He kept thinking about the letter.

The gun sounded in the relay. Skip couldn't concentrate. His mind was first on the letter, then on the relay, imagining that he would have a lead, then lose it.

His teammate was rounding the backstretch, in the lead. Skip reached for the baton, felt it, and closed his hand around it.

He ran in the lead, thanks to his teammate. The crowd on the infield yelled in his ear. He couldn't make out the words. They were just sounds, but the noise added to his confusion.

Skip tried to think of the race, tried to pace himself. He maintained the lead going into the third curve, the 330 mark.

Going into the last 100 yards, he had settled down and was talking to himself, telling himself to push his legs, to run faster.

Then he heard feet behind him. And the slight breeze that he always felt when someone passed him.

He passed off the baton. Pushing through the crowd to the back of the stands, he looked back to see his teammate losing more distance.

He had lost the lead and the relay on his leg. Humiliation and anger overwhelmed him. He had been pulled from the 880. His race. He could have won that one. Certainly placed. That would have been enough.

At fifteen, his whole world was suddenly shattering again. He found a spot behind the bleachers and cried. No one had to tell him that he hadn't lettered. He knew.

He had come so close to leaving disappointment and frustration behind. At that moment, he wasn't sure he had the spirit to try anything else again.

6

Hurdles in the Hall

The rhythmic hum of the ambulance's tires kept Skip in a state of pleasant drowsiness as they rolled toward Woodrow Wilson. He slowly turned the collection of athletic memories in his mind, as if he were turning a globe to view a different part of the world.

His failure to win a letter hadn't been the end of his young world. The summer sun had quickly bronzed him and burned away the disappointment of the track season. He spent his vacation running, working with weights, surfing, and waterskiing.

When he returned in the fall of 1965 for his junior year at Princess Anne High School and another try at football, he was named the No. 2 left halfback. He became the starter in the second game.

The third game of the season remained one of his happiest memories. Princess Anne had the ball for its second series of downs in the first quarter. Skip caught a flare pass in the left flat near the line of scrimmage. He dug his cleats into the ground, pushed off, and sped upfield. He changed direction at nearly full speed to evade one defensive back, repelled the safety man with a stiff-arm, and outran two trailing defenders into the end zone. It was his first touchdown as a varsity player.

The score represented a breakthrough. With it, he gained a confidence that had been lacking before. He began to relax with his teammates, joining in the jokes and the locker-room kidding.

He ended the season as the team's leading rusher. He had become a threat on the sweeps and through the line. The newspapers referred to him as an "elusive, dazzling, open-field runner."

Shortly after the season ended, he received letters from three universities. Each said that he had the potential to play football in college and each expressed an interest in him, saying that he would be watched closely in his senior year.

His newfound confidence went with him into track season. He ran the 880 and the mile relay, lettering in indoor track in the winter and in spring track.

In his senior year, he was named the starting left halfback. The team's offense was built around him and Charlie Shea, the fullback. More colleges began sending word through his coach, John Grady, that they were interested in him.

Even a sprained ankle, suffered in a pileup in the first game, didn't deter him. For the next three days, he watched every practice, leaning on a crutch. On Thursday, the day before the second game, he was able to put weight on the ankle. For the next twenty-four hours, he would one moment accept the fact that he wouldn't be able to play and, in the next moment, make up his mind to try it.

He showed up Friday evening in the locker room still not sure what to do. But the preparations for the game infected him. He wanted to play. He dressed for the game and ran several sets of sprints to convince the team doctor and the coach that the ankle was strong. It screamed with pain as he ran the sprints, but he was careful not to favor it.

He acted his way through the warmups and watched unhappily from the bench as Princess Anne bogged down on the first series of downs and punted.

On the second series, he was sent in with a trap play; he was to get the ball. As he ran toward the huddle, he kept reminding himself that the slightest indication of a limp would return him to the bench. He gave no evidence of the pain that he felt with each step.

As soon as he felt that ball slammed into his stomach, he drove for the hole that had been opened. He cut hard on the injured

ankle toward the sideline as soon as he crossed the line of scrimmage. In the secondary, he dodged two defensive backs and had a
clear field ahead of him.

For the remaining 45 yards, his gait alternated from a fluid run
to a hobble as the pain drove itself up his leg and into his head. He
crossed the goal line and let the ball drop to the ground. He
limped back to the bench and the anguish on his face told Coach
Grady and the doctor that he wouldn't play again that night.

Even with the sensitive ankle in the early games, Skip established himself as the premier running back for Princess Anne.

The team had won five consecutive games and Skip had scored
six touchdowns and was the leading ground-gainer as Princess
Anne readied for the final game of his senior year.

The seniors were keyed up in the locker room before the game
with Cox High School. Skip was saddened at the prospect of not
playing again with the teammates who had become such close
friends during the past two seasons. He was, at the same time,
priming himself to give this game everything that he could give.
He didn't worry about the possibility of an injury. This was it. The
last game of his high school career.

He scored twice in the first quarter, taking the ball in from the
Cox 5-yard line for the first touchdown and outracing the secondary for a 35-yard score on the second touchdown.

Before the third quarter had ended, he had scored two more
touchdowns, one on a 59-yard run that brought the Princess
Anne fans to their feet, screaming for him to go all the way as he
displayed his finest example of broken-field running. His last
score came on a 10-yard pass. He had carried the ball nine times
for 140 yards and ended his senior year with sixty points. Days
later the statistics showed that he was the fifth highest scorer in
the district. He was named to the all-district team.

The colleges started to woo him in earnest when the season
ended. He received letters from twenty colleges and universities.
All requested that he consider playing football for them.

College representatives began paying calls on Skip. Frequently he was summoned out of class to meet with them in the athletic office. All had heard or read about him; some had scouted him. They all wanted him.

But they wanted something else, too, and that was a problem. Skip's grades were a solid C average, but he hadn't done well enough on the College Boards to meet the entrance requirements for many of the colleges. Several of the representatives counseled Skip to spend the next year in a prep school, where he could beef up his grades and continue to develop his athletic ability.

He discussed the situation with his parents and decided to enroll at Frederick Military Academy in nearby Portsmouth in the event that his approaching final try at the College Boards didn't improve his standing.

Shortly after football had ended, Skip added two events to his contributions to the indoor track team. They came about by accident. The team had been working out inside the school building during a cold and rainy afternoon. During a lull in the exercises, Skip approached and cleared a high hurdle that had been set up in the long hallway. Coach Grady had turned a corner of the hallway in time to see Skip clear the barrier with remarkable ease.

He asked Skip to try it again.

Skip walked back to his starting point, bent down in his starting stance, and again cleared the hurdle. He showed good form as well as speed.

Coach Grady set up a full flight of hurdles in the hall. Before the afternoon was over, Skip had become a high hurdler for Princess Anne in addition to a competitor in the pole vault, the high jump, long jump, 50-yard dash and relay. His natural ability in the hurdles showed and he began winning.

When he also entered the low hurdles for the first time in the high school's district meet, he set records in both the high and low hurdles.

He co-captained the spring track team, leading it to first place in the city meet when he won the high and low hurdles.

His abilities on the football field and on the track caught the attention of Red Wilson, the newly appointed football coach at Elon College, a small four-year institution outside Burlington, North Carolina.

The coach offered him a scholarship which would continue each year if Skip could maintain a C average once he enrolled. Skip accepted the offer and withdrew his application to Frederick.

Princess Anne High School's awards ceremony, three days before graduation, crowned Skip's final year at school. In front of the whole student body, assembled in the football stadium, Skip was called forward to accept the trophy as the school's Athlete of the Year.

The determination and work had paid off.

Graduation ceremonies were more important to his parents than to Skip. He was restless as he waited in line with his fellow seniors to march into the stadium on Friday night. Ahead was a two-day trip to North Carolina's Outer Banks and some of the best surfing on the East Coast.

As the line began to shuffle forward, and Skip moved toward the seats set up in the center of the field, he became sad.

The feeling was sudden and totally unexpected. When he crossed the football field, the memories of the games, his runs, his pass receptions, and the friendships that had been born and had grown in the locker room filled his mind. For the first time, he realized that this night ended the happiest year of his life in athletics.

He tried to concentrate on the speaker's words, but his thoughts returned to football and track. He looked toward the bleachers, jammed with parents. His eyes sought out the cinder track, hardly visible in the deep shadows caused by the floodlights. He pictured himself, left arm and right leg extended forward, parallel to the ground, clearing a high hurdle. The excitement about college turned into a pinprick fright. He won-

dered whether he would be as good in college as he had been at
Princess Anne.

"Alfred T. Wilkins, Jr." The name boomed out of the loud-
speakers and spread throughout the stadium. He watched his
classmates, one by one, mount the platform and receive their
diplomas. He hadn't heard the first name called. And now his
name was being shouted, it seemed to him. Before the last sound
of the "r" in "Jr." had drifted into silence, he heard a collection of
cheers, screams, and yells from a section of the bleachers. He
could recognize Linda's voice above the others. There they were
once again, he thought, as he made his way toward the platform.
His cheering section. The family that urged him on, encouraged
him when he was hurt and low and teased him back to humility
when he acted cocky and smug. He mounted the steps and strode
toward the principal who held the diploma in his outstretched
hand.

As Skip walked toward the other end of the platform to return
to his seat he could hear Linda's voice, now clear above the polite
clapping of the others in the bleachers, and the small, tight knot
of Wilkinses who were clapping louder and harder and longer
than anyone else.

The rest of graduation night became a series of pleasant de-
tours on the way to the Outer Banks. The seniors lingered after
the ceremony, seeking out those who had been closest to them,
embracing, shaking hands, offering good wishes.

Skip and his friend Gary O'Brien stopped at Skip's home
where the Wilkins family was waiting with cake and more good
wishes. Patsy Wilkins urged Skip and Gary to stay the night and
drive to the Outer Banks the next morning.

"Mom," Skip said, with a newfound sense of independence,
"you've helped me live my life for seventeen years. I'm taking
over."

Tommy Wilkins smiled at both of them.

"He's right, Patsy. It's time. He's on his own now."

Those words jolted Skip into the realization that he was riding
in an ambulance, on his back, paralyzed—no longer on his own.

He wished alternately that the driver would hurry and reach their destination or that by some magic, something would happen to snatch him out of this bad dream, that he and his parents would suddenly find themselves at home and that everything would be normal.

But there wasn't any magic and the ambulance continued on the two-hundred-mile trip to Fishersville and Woodrow Wilson Rehabilitation Center.

Part II

Part II

7

I'm Skip from Virginia Beach

The sunshine and the slight warm breeze felt good on my face as I waited for the stretcher to be pushed inside.

The building in front of me wasn't impressive; it was old and the brick was dulled.

But I was, in a way, excited to be at Woodrow Wilson. This was the place where I was going to walk again. I was anxious to get started. Whenever the word "rehabilitation" had been mentioned to me in Norfolk General, I had a vision of a stationary bicycle—the kind used for exercise, with no front wheel. I could see doctors and nurses helping me onto the seat, then working my feet and my legs so that the pedals began to turn. Then I would start learning how to make my legs work without help. I was prepared for it to take a while, but I knew that I would learn to walk again.

My excitement and expectations vanished as soon as I was rolled inside. The hallway was dimly lit and cool, almost cold. The walls were cinderblock, yellowed with age and badly scuffed. The odor of urine and the heavy scent of disinfectant became stronger and stronger as we proceeded down the hall toward a room that would be my new home. I passed a dozen men, old and young, black and white. They had one thing in common: all were in wheelchairs. They looked at me as I was rolled by, but none of them spoke. There was no exchange of greetings, no acknowledgement of one another.

Even before I reached my room I was becoming confused, but

the room and its sparse furniture pushed me past confusion and into fright. I wasn't going to be in a private room anymore. I wasn't going to have the individual attention that I had received in Norfolk. My bed was one of nine. They were olive green, mostly chipped and scratched. No buttons raised and lowered the bed. A single hand crank was at the foot of each. There was no radio. No television. No button to call a nurse.

How was I expected to learn to walk again in such a place?

My mind reeled at my surroundings when an orderly ushered my parents out of the room and stood over me as I lay in bed.

His voice was friendly.

"Well, let's see here, my man. We got to get you dressed so you can tour this place."

Dressed? I hadn't been dressed since the accident. And I'd refused to let Mom pack any of my good clothes. Somehow the clothes that I had taken so much pride in didn't seem right for the way I looked. *Why does he want to dress me anyway,* I wondered, *just to sit in a wheelchair?* I didn't ask or argue. I was too overwhelmed by this new place.

He peeled off my T-shirt and asked me if I wanted to put on underwear. He answered his own question, not waiting for me. "No, I doubt you do. Nobody in the infirmary does. It's a hassle. Especially when you have an accident." No underwear.

He pulled and pushed my limbs and rolled my body back and forth as he needed, bent and shoved each leg into a pair of pants and hiked the pants up to my waist. He explained everything he was doing to me as he worked. His words didn't register. I was sure he didn't know what he was doing. I was afraid that he was going to break my neck again. I'd never been treated that way.

After he had gotten my pants up and zipped, another attendant appeared. They turned me and partially lifted me into my four-poster brace. They quickly and casually tightened the brace and then lifted me out of bed and into a wheelchair. Just the two of them. In Norfolk, at least three and sometimes four attendants were needed to transfer me.

As soon as they had released me, I gasped for breath. The

brace was too high and it forced my head back. The chair had a straight back, not a slanted one. The combination of the brace and the pressure of sitting upright for the first time began to choke off my breath.

I was struggling for air and fighting back tears. There was no way that I could survive, let alone get well, if this was going to be my treatment. *I'll never do it,* I thought. *It's all over.*

I didn't want to cry. I had been working to be calm. But the tears came. I lost my control and my ability to fight my feelings and I wept. My first time sitting up in this place and all I could do was weep.

The attendants, in gentle tones, tried to calm me. One of them quickly and easily readjusted the brace. The other kept patting my shoulder and telling me that everything was going to be all right.

Gradually I regained my breath and my composure. I was thankful that none of the family had seen me.

The tour of the center did little to lessen my apprehension. The rest of the main building and its furnishings were in the same state of disrepair as my room and my bed. There were three new buildings—a dormitory for vocational students, a dining hall, and the recreation center with a swimming pool and television lounge. The family focused their conversation and excitement on the new things. We were all trying very hard to be encouraging and optimistic.

My introduction to the center left me weak and exhausted. In the first hour, I had been dressed for the first time since the accident; I had been forced to sit absolutely upright for the first time since the accident; and I had been bent, twisted, pushed, and pulled as though there were nothing wrong with me.

I was back in bed trying to collect my thoughts when the door opened. I looked up to see a fully clothed young man push his wheelchair into the room. We were alone and we looked awkwardly at each other for a moment.

"Hi, you're the new man, huh?" he said, rolling closer to the side of my bed.

I couldn't take my eyes off him. He was a contradiction in this new environment. This place was supposed to help people get well. Yet here was a man, fully dressed and managing for himself and *still* in a wheelchair.

"Yeah, my name's Skip Wilkins. I'm from Virginia Beach. Why are you in that wheelchair?" The question came out before I meant to ask it.

He looked puzzled. "What do you mean? I broke my back."

"How long ago?"

"Five years."

I didn't understand. In a split second, I had asked another question, but it was a question that I really didn't want answered.

"Five years? And you're not out of that wheelchair yet? What's the matter with you?"

He looked at me as if I were crazy. That was his only response.

He rolled out and left me once again with my thoughts and the growing vision of my future.

Why hadn't this place helped him to walk again?

Was I going to be in a wheelchair for the rest of my life?

I had thought often about the accident. I had acknowledged that my injury was serious. I had watched my once active and obviously muscular body deteriorate. But I had not really accepted the possibility of being permanently crippled.

Now, with that young man, it was different. It was believable. There was a person who had been injured, had been in rehabilitation, and he was still in a wheelchair five years later. Five years or perhaps forever. Maybe it was just a matter of time until I had to face the fact that I would always be in a wheelchair, but at that moment I wished I could escape, could leave, could run away. But I couldn't. The place itself was forcing me to accept the idea of life as a cripple. If I could leave, get to a new and better place, I could get well.

My eyes began to fill with tears and the tears, for the second time that day, were ready to flood. But I wouldn't give in this time. I couldn't give up. I had to try. Maybe I would be different. Maybe I would learn to walk again.

The door opened and a large black man, dressed in a uniform so small that the buttons strained, came in. He was pushing a young man in a chair. As they passed, both spoke.

"Hello there. I'm Junior," the black man said with a smile. "And this here, this is Tommy."

Tommy, a nice-looking, frail boy about my age, nodded shyly.

"I'm Skip. From Virginia Beach."

Before we exchanged any more information, Junior said he'd be back to me after he put Tommy in bed.

I smiled for the first time. With just a few words, Junior had introduced himself as a nice man.

He began the same procedure on Tommy that I had experienced when returned to bed. As I watched, I began to understand that Tommy's situation was like mine—he needed the same kind of help. Yet with him, the effort seemed to be part of a pattern; not awkward or embarrassing or frightening as it had been to me.

Watching brought some relief to me and the hope that maybe I, too, could relax and let the tugging and the pulling become part of a routine.

But as quickly as I tried to make myself comfortable with that idea, I had a terrifying thought. Someone was going to have to take care of me for the rest of my life. No, I told myself. No. As soon as that thought tried to return, I found something new in the room to study or to think about, forcing myself away from the negative idea.

Every time I came close to getting a grip on myself, persuading myself that I had to fight back and I had to try, I met a new obstacle. A young girl who helped out at the center fed me supper. It was obvious that she hadn't dealt with a newcomer before and I had no strength to help and no knowledge of what to do. She shoveled forkful after forkful of food at me, jamming the utensils so deeply into my throat that I gagged and the mashed potatoes oozed out of the sides of my mouth and down onto my chest. I became sick thinking of the sloppiness of the situation and the helplessness of my condition. I made a promise to myself right then that I would learn quickly to eat without help.

Shortly after supper, I became thirsty. A plastic jug filled with crushed ice and water was on my nightstand. I had not fed myself anything except grapes since the accident, but I decided to begin to learn. Besides, there was no one to help me.

It took a long time to lift the jar to my chest and to maneuver it close to my mouth.

Just as I thought that I was about to succeed in my first effort to help myself, the bottom of the jar slipped backward on my chest, pouring the contents over me and the bed.

I had an awful sensation. I could see the mound of ice on my stomach and the large wet areas on my T-shirt. But I couldn't feel the wetness or the cold. I wanted to move, to get up, to get out from under the mess even though I couldn't feel anything. Again, as my mind told my body to get up and nothing happened, I was reminded that I was paralyzed.

Junior came in and cut short any further self-pity.

"Damn, boy. Will you look at that? You ain't been here a whole day yet and you already causin' trouble." His tone let me know he wasn't upset. I wondered how he could have so much patience. I managed a weak smile and he smiled back.

"I'll be right back and we'll get it cleaned up. Better not be long 'fore you're drainin' that jug without spillin' a drop."

Those words, spoken by this big man whom I had known only a couple of hours, gave me hope. I had tried something on my own. I had failed, but he was telling me that eventually I'd succeed. And he was pulling for me to keep trying.

The next afternoon I met Chris Smith. I immediately had a warm feeling about him. I had heard about Chris before I got to the center. He was from Portsmouth, near Virginia Beach, and he, too, had a broken neck. His injury happened while he was roughhousing after a touch football game.

Chris looked comfortable in his chair. Unlike some of the other patients I had seen, he had neatly cut, clean hair and was clean shaven. His clothes fit him well. His shoes were tied.

We chatted for a few minutes and then he rolled toward the door. Before he went out, he turned back to me.

"Hey, Skip, take it easy for a while. I'll see you later and we'll see if we can't get our beds put next to each other."

He smiled and lifted his hand as high as he could in a wave and was gone.

But he left something that was important to me. He left me the feeling that I had been accepted by someone else in this strange and still-frightening world and that he was going to be my friend. Now I had two friends—Chris and Junior. That thought didn't stay with me long after Chris left the room, but it represented a forward step simply because I allowed it at all. *Hey*, I thought, *maybe this isn't going to be so bad after all.*

Mom, Dad, and my grandparents left me that afternoon. It was probably because I had just met Chris that I had a little confidence when they came to my bed to tell me good-bye. I was trying to view my stay at the center as a stay at football training camp, trying to make a team. I didn't know exactly what I was going to do at the center, but I was going to do whatever I was asked.

Dad told me that the doctor had asked them not to come back to visit for a while. I started telling myself that when they did return I would be different—stronger and able to do some things.

"Now you call Granny and Papa and your mom and me at least once a week," Dad said. "We'll write and we'll be up as soon as possible. You can do it, Skip," he told me.

None of us that day knew what "it" would entail.

Mom leaned down and kissed my cheek. "I'll pray for you, Skippy. And remember, God is with you."

It was a good parting. When they left, I felt excited about what lay ahead. I was beginning to understand that I had an uphill and pretty steep climb ahead of me, but I was determined to fight as hard and as long as I had to.

I was taken to X-ray on Monday. Dr. O'Hanlan, the senior doctor on the center's staff, wanted to see for himself the damage to my neck. After he analyzed the films, he told me that my neck was in a stable condition and that I didn't need to wear the brace or even the collar.

I proudly relayed the news in my first phone call home.

The absence of the brace combined with the straight back of the wheelchair caused me to pass out the next time I was transferred to the chair. I hadn't had to learn, until then, how to breathe from my diaphragm. Without the brace to elevate my head and without the tilt to the back of the chair to keep the pressure off my diaphragm, I couldn't get air. My body adjusted quickly and when I regained consciousness, I was breathing without difficulty.

That same day I learned more about the importance of encouragement. I was sitting in a regular wheelchair with pegs on the rims. An attendant explained to me that my hands, despite their lifeless fingers, could pressure the pegs and turn the wheels. My first effort moved the chair from the bed to the door, about twenty feet. It veered sharply to the left because I had more strength on my right side.

Still, those few feet represented a big step forward.

The attendant patted me on the shoulder.

"That's great, Skip. That's just great. You'll be up and down these halls in no time." He said it in a way that made me want to succeed for him as well as for myself.

I quickly got into a routine at Fishersville. I went to physical therapy each morning. At first I spent my time being strapped down and angled into various positions on a tilt board to rebuild my circulation. Then I began to develop and train and challenge the muscles that I still had to their full usefulness.

I had occupational therapy in the afternoon. I began to learn new and different ways of performing the simplest acts of living. In my second session, the therapist fixed a strap around the palm of my hand. There was a slit in the strap that helped me to hold a pen or pencil or fork. Before the end of my first week, I had managed to type a brief letter to my parents, using the unsharpened end of a pencil to depress the typewriter keys.

As quickly as I learned to perform a basic function—eating with a spoon or fork, brushing my teeth, combing my hair—another challenge, always a little more difficult than the last one, awaited me—transferring from the chair to the bed, partially dressing myself. In each new task, I left behind as many of the medical aids and devices as I could.

The vision of the exercise bicycle that was going to help me walk again blurred and gradually disappeared. It was replaced by the reality of small weights that had to be lifted, of an object that had to be held.

Many of the everyday activities, like the morning and afternoon therapy, became agreeable patterns in my life. Other things, however, were hard to accept.

None of us received much personal attention because of the vastness of the center and the small number of attendants and orderlies. I realized that there couldn't be much attention, but understanding it didn't diminish the desire for it.

Morning preparations for the nine of us in our one room were handled in mechanical fashion. There was only so much time to dress each patient and only so much time to help each patient groom himself. If I decided to stay in bed past the scheduled time to get up, I would lie in my bed, alone in the room for hours until someone found the time to help just me.

There was no privacy, not even for the most personal needs. Bowel training was accomplished in front of everyone in the room. My first experience was degrading and repulsive. It never changed. Four or five of us lay naked on our bed pads while we were helped, by medication and attendants, to eliminate our waste. I clenched my teeth and squeezed my eyes shut as hard as I could. I was trying to shut out the reality of what was happening to me, with me and around me. Whenever the day came for the program, I had to talk to myself to get through it. Such things I came to accept as necessary, but I couldn't handle them without enormous mental effort.

8

The World Doesn't Owe You Anything

As I struggled to overcome my fear and confusion during those first days in the center, I began to think about God. I knew enough from my upbringing to believe that God existed. I had been told over and over by my parents, beginning in the emergency room the day of the accident, that God would help me. I decided that I needed to establish a relationship with him because I desperately needed help.

I made a commitment to him, promising that I would pray to him daily and would read his Word if he would help me get better.

I thought I was willing to do anything to get well. So I tried to live up to my commitment. I got out the Bible that my parents had given me as a child and started at the first page. I read and reread the story of the Creation and other passages, the same stories that I'd been told in Sunday school. They bored me. I kept trying, but something was lacking. Maybe my desire wasn't strong enough. Maybe I didn't understand how to go about what I had promised him I would do. I began to feel that I was letting him down, so I decided that the best thing for me to do was not to bother him at all, though I somehow always knew he was with me. I just didn't know how to reach out.

I wasn't able to draw strength from God, but I did find strength in some people. Chris became an important person in my life. He was more severely injured than I. He had no movement in his arms and wrists. I, at least, had some arm and shoulder movement and some strength in my wrists. He was a constant reminder that I could have been much worse off. He gave me something more important, however, than feeling thankful for my condition. He had learned to be positive about his future. He had learned to try and never give up. Because I knew that I had more use of my body than he, I always tried harder.

As Chris and I became closer through the weeks, we discovered that we had something very special in common. He had developed a strong relationship, outside of the center, with one of the therapists. I had become attracted to Sally, who was in charge of my occupational therapy.

Even at the outset of the therapy sessions, her encouragement was important to me. I wanted to please her. I soon began to feel that she was interested in me as a person as well as in my development as a patient. She frequently spent more time working with me, staying closer to me than to the other patients. Her smiles of approval to me seemed warmer than those to the others. She often would give me a pat of encouragement or put her arm around my shoulders and hug me after I had accomplished some therapy task.

After a surprise party on my eighteenth birthday when the others had left the therapy room, Sally gave me a present. Then she kissed me. It wasn't just a friendly birthday kiss. Sally was an attractive female and I began to realize, because of the way she apparently felt about me, that I still had emotions and I still wanted to be cared about and loved.

We began to spend time together away from the center. We enjoyed being with each other, we enjoyed the touch of one another and, as the relationship deepened, we kissed and embraced on our dates away from the center. I don't know that Sally and I were in love, but I know that we did have serious emotional and physical feelings for each other. Finally, though, her internship at Woodrow Wilson ended and she left to work in another part of Virginia.

We knew that we would probably not see each other again, but our mutual feelings marked an important part of my rehabilitation: I began to believe in myself as a person; I began to believe that I could be attractive to other people again.

Granny and Papa always had been special to me. They often gave me and my sisters the little extras that Mom and Dad could not afford. Their visits to see me at Fishersville deepened my appreciation of them. Their hearts went out to those around me as much as to me. When they went to Rowe's Steak House for a surprise steak for me, they came back with steaks for others. It became a gentle joke among the patients: "I'm hungry. When are Granny and Papa coming to visit?" It had to be expensive, but they never stopped the practice. Their visits always meant some of Granny's homemade chicken and rolls—for the entire room, of course.

My ability to type a letter, punching one letter and then another with the pencil, gave me a special connection with Karen and Shirley. They wrote to me in the large scrawling hand of their age and I wrote back on the typewriter. It gave me the feeling of being a big brother away at college.

By the end of August, I was feeding myself and gaining weight. I even went to the circus the second week in September. Then, on September 21, I suffered a setback.

I had started on bladder training to end my need for a catheter, which drained into a plastic bag clipped to my right side. Once I succeeded with the training, the catheter would be replaced by a snuggly fitting rubber sheath with a tube running to the leg bag. The catheter, because it was a foreign object inserted inside my penis, represented a constant potential for bacteria and urinary tract infections.

The training seemed simple when it was explained to me. The doctor would remove the catheter. I would be required to drink at least eight ounces of water each hour that I was awake. I was shown how to hit myself in the bladder area; the slight blow would trigger the bladder, forcing it to empty completely and properly.

When I actually practiced what I had been told, it didn't work. I forced more liquids. Within a short time, my bladder started to swell, pushing itself against my stomach. My stomach became distended. My repeated blows to my bladder area failed to make me void. Within hours, I had fire-red splotches over my body. I became chilled, then I broke out in sweat from the internal sickness. I ran a fever.

I had to stop and the catheter had to be reinserted. I tried again the next day, and the next, without success. The constant failures to train my bladder were slowly causing uremic poisoning.

The poisoning finally made itself obvious. A high fever developed that didn't break, even with the catheter reinserted. I was taken from the center to the hospital at Staunton where I was packed in an ice bath until the fever dropped. Then came minor surgery to crush the kidney stones that had developed in my bladder.

When I returned to the center, I tried the bladder training program again. Again it failed. For the next several weeks, I was in and out of hospitals: first at Staunton, then at the University of Virginia Hospital in Charlottesville.

I was caught in a horrible medical dilemma. I needed to train my bladder in order for them to remove the catheter and its potential for disease, but each effort at training brought on uremic poisoning.

The feeling of helplessness and frustration came back. I had fought so hard to get better, to take care of myself. The sickness stopped my progress. I wondered whether I had anything left to give. And yet, each time I asked the question, I looked at others who had so much less than I did and I thought of my family and how much it would mean to them for me to get better. Somehow, I was able to dig deeper inside and try again.

At Thanksgiving, I went home for the first time. Mom and Dad had worked to make everything just right. Dad had built a small ramp at the front door for the wheelchair. Linda had moved all of her belongings upstairs to my old room, Karen and Shirley had moved into Linda's room, and Mom and Dad had taken the two girls' room. I was given my parents' first-floor bedroom, the largest in the house. It had been completely furnished by our longtime friend, Leonard Strelitz, who owned a furniture outlet store.

Dad had hung pictures of my football and track performances on the wall.

Karen and Shirley were my constant companions. I wasn't able to pull myself up in bed or do much else without help, so they stayed with me, waiting on me and watching television with me. Their attention made me feel that they had missed me and needed me as much as I missed and needed them.

Linda was in and out of the house with her own social life, but she would always stop by before going out or come in to see me after her dates and tell me where she'd been and whom she'd seen.

But my homecoming was not the happy occasion we had anticipated. I felt awkward. At Fishersville I was like the others. At home the people were different. They could walk. When I went home I realized that Mom and Dad would probably have to do all the things for me that attendants did at the center. They had already done so much. Yet there was so much ahead for them to do, no matter how much better I became.

Martha Chevalier, who I had been dating before the accident, came over to talk to me almost as soon as I arrived. She looked great. I had written her several times from Fishersville. She had always responded quickly, telling me how much she wanted to see me when I came home. Her letters were friendly and mostly filled with news about what she was doing and questions about me. But I didn't know how she would react to me in a wheelchair.

While I was home, I was invited to a party for the football team. She came to the house to visit after the party. Because of my experience with Sally, I continued to hope that one day I would have a relationship with someone. Someone like Sally or Martha. We didn't talk that night about seeing each other in the future, but I felt that she wanted to be with me. Our letters became longer and more frequent when I went back to Fishersville.

Mike Whitley, the friend who had helped with outdoor household chores after the accident, had an older brother, Wayne. Wayne was also at the party. He had played tackle on the football team and had been one of my classmates, but we hadn't been too close. During Thanksgiving he came by the house several times and we kidded and talked about football. He came to visit, I suspect, because he was something of a loner and he knew I'd become something of a loner too.

When I returned home for Christmas, Martha, Wayne, and Mike were the first people to visit. Martha and I dated during Christmas in the only way that I could. She visited in the evenings and had dinner with the family. We would watch television and talk in the privacy of my room.

Wayne borrowed football films of the games in my senior year and brought them over. As I watched myself on the screen, healthy, strong and running, the question of playing again kept coming back to me. I kept answering the question no, but I still hoped, without reason, that my athletic career wasn't over.

Except for the visits from Martha, Wayne, and Mike, Christmas was a sad time. Our family tried hard to make the holiday as much like past Christmases as they could. But we tried too hard. The strain, especially on Mom, was beginning to surface. After we opened our presents on Christmas morning, an awkwardness filled the house. All of us knew that, because of the concern about too much activity for me, we would not be riding to Papa's for a traditional Christmas Day breakfast and more presents. I couldn't take my mind off the thought that my presence had brought an end to one of our most cherished times as a family. I tried to be happy and lighthearted, but I kept thinking about the burden I had become. Christmas of 1967 was the worst Christmas that we had ever had.

I returned to Fishersville to resume my therapy. The center had halted my bladder training after the repeated failures and the repeated fevers and trips to area hospitals. I remained on the catheter.

Dad called in the spring with a possible solution to the problem. He had located a Norfolk urologist, Eugene Poutasse, who had practiced in rehabilitation centers and had successfully performed the required surgery many times. I had known for some time that Dad had been trying to find a doctor but I never thought about it. I had begun to dislike hospitals. And I had almost come to accept the fact that I would need to have a catheter, with its potential for problems, for the rest of my life.

I left Woodrow Wilson Rehabilitation Center on June 1, 1968, nine months after the ambulance from Norfolk General had stopped outside the dull brick building in Fishersville, Virginia, that had become my world.

I didn't know whether or not I would return as a patient. The decision would be based on the success of the scheduled bladder operation and how well I could get along at home.

As I was preparing to leave, Robert Smith, one of the older patients who had been in and out of the center for thirteen years, spoke words I didn't want to hear.

"Skip," he said, "be prepared to make new friends when you get home. Your old friends' lives have gone on since you came here and they won't be there to help you pick up your life."

I argued with him.

"You don't know how many friends I have. They'll be there to help."

A sadness came to his face and he gently shook his head.

"I hope so, Skip. I sure hope so."

Dr. O'Hanlan saw me shortly before I left and gave me the same kind of advice.

"Skip, you have a lot of potential. But you've got to remember one thing, if you don't come back here: be prepared to change for the world. Because the world won't change for you. It doesn't owe you anything."

His words were hard, too. They tempered my happiness at being discharged. But, there were definitely reasons to be happy. Physically, I was stronger. I had gained back twenty-five pounds and weighed 145.

I was able to partially dress myself.

I could feed myself.

I was able to push my chair, to get around on level surfaces.

Mentally, I was able to acknowledge my present limitations. I continued to hope for a way to improve, but I recognized that I was bound, at least for a while longer, to a wheelchair.

I didn't want to accept the counsel that I had been given, but I had learned that Dr. O'Hanlan knew a lot about people in my condition. I filed away his words, hoping that I wouldn't need to be reminded of them.

The operation on the bladder was called a TUR—transurethral resection. It required trimming some of the muscle out of the neck of the bladder so that the muscle would respond to internal or external pressure, such as the blows that I had been instructed to deliver to myself.

I woke in my room after surgery and looked down at the urine bag clamped to the side of the bed.

The bag was nearly filled with blood-tinted liquid. Dr. Poutasse came in and assured me that everything had gone well.

Days later the catheter that had been inserted following the surgery was removed and I again was put on a training program. Dad sat beside me in the hospital room as I drank cup after cup of water.

The symptoms that I had come to recognize so well began to return. My bladder started to distend once more. I began to splotch. I could feel myself getting warm, then hot. I broke into patches of sweat. I hit my bladder area over and over. Nothing happened. I was becoming panicky.

Nurses put me in a tub of warm water. Still nothing happened. Finally they put me back in bed.

"I'm afraid we'll have to put the catheter back in," one of them said.

When they left, I told Dad that I wanted to try something.

"Dad, I don't want that catheter back in. Come over here and press down real hard on my bladder. I saw it done at the center."

He was hesitant at first.

"Where? What do you mean, Skip?"

I explained as well as I could.

"I've got to somehow trigger my bladder off. You push down real hard on my stomach." I showed him where.

"How hard?"

"Hard. Right here."

He pushed.

I felt a sensation inside my body.

"Push again. Harder."

He put one knee on the bed beside me and pressed again.

Fluid, a mixture of blood and urine, trickled out. We both saw it.

"Push again."

He did. This time the urge to void gave way to another trickle. Then a stream.

I was voiding. I mean *really* voiding.

The two of us must have looked ridiculous.

We didn't feel ridiculous, though. We both knew what had happened. The operation had worked; with practice I would be able to trigger the emptying of my bladder and to leave behind the catheter, one of the morbid reminders of my condition. I would be fitted with an external device which had no perils of infection or discomfort.

One of the nurses returned to the room. Before she could take in the sight and understand what had happened, I told her that she wouldn't need to bring the catheter.

9

Prepare for the Future

I was home and there were no problems staring me in the face. The nine months at Fishersville had helped me develop my muscles and my ability to get along with little assistance. The stay at the center also had built my determination to tackle yet unforeseen obstacles. My emotional outlook was healthy.

During my first weeks at Fishersville, I had built up a fear of coming home. I worried about the things that Mom and Dad would have to do for me the rest of my life. Only days after I came home from the TUR operation, that fear was completely erased by the way Mom and Dad had handled my needs. At first, Dad had been the one to help dress and undress me. Mom had watched. Then, Mom had begun to assist. Now she had assumed the full responsibility, freeing Dad during the week to concentrate on his job. The changing of roles had been so gradual and so smooth that I hardly noticed. Mom and I were comfortable working together each morning and evening.

Wayne Whitley's visits during June represented some of the best medicine that I received. He treated me as though nothing had happened to me and always encouraged me to go out with him to visit and be together with other people.

One afternoon in late June, I overheard Mom talking on the telephone. She was telling someone that she couldn't leave the house. Only Shirley and Karen were home and there was no way that I could be put into the car to ride with her.

When she hung up, I rolled into the room.

"Mom, come on. I can go with you."

"Skippy," she said, "you know I can't lift you. Even with the girls' help. You can't get into the car."

"I watched a lot of people at Fishersville getting in and out of cars without being lifted. We'll put my transfer board on the car seat and I'll just slide from the chair into the car. Then we can leave the chair here. Come on, let's try it."

She thought about it for a moment, then smiled.

"OK, if you think we can."

I told Mom and Shirley and Karen what to do, remembering the transfers I'd seen at the center. The girls slid one end of the long narrow piece of wood under my chair seat and rested the other end on the car seat. I was awkward and slow; I had never tried to transfer without the help of someone, like Dad, who could lift my weight. Slowly, putting weight on my knuckles and arms, I was able to shift my body along the board while the girls held the board. Finally I rested, somewhat awkwardly, on the car seat. Mom lifted my legs into the car and Shirley and Karen put the wheelchair in the house.

As the Volkswagen pulled away from the house, I left behind one more barrier. That day we won my freedom to travel, a freedom that had become precious to me only when it was no longer mine.

Linda, now seventeen, became my chauffeur, and all three sisters became my constant companions and my closest friends during the summer. We drove to the beach nearly every day. The heat was a problem for me because my body no longer adjusted to it. I could perspire only in response to sickness, not external heat. I passed out several times before we learned to carry water and ice with us. We always went to the beach near a place that offered me air conditioning if I became too hot in the sun. Shirley and Karen would push me along the boardwalk or sit with me inside a restaurant or snack bar when the temperature forced me out of the sun.

August brought with it another effort by Dad to find a way to help me. He and Leonard Strelitz had been working to have me evaluated at the highly acclaimed Albert Einstein Institute in New York City. Dad was determined to try anything available to help me.

Dad told me that the doctors at Albert Einstein Institute had made a preliminary study of my records. They thought there might be a bone chip pressuring my spine that could be removed. If that were true, I might regain the use of some of my muscles.

I had mixed emotions as I prepared for the trip. So much had happened to me in the past year. So many ups, so many downs. Every time hope for a normal life appeared, I came out of the situation with new evidence that my life in a wheelchair would be permanent.

But I kept on hoping. Maybe someone, somewhere would be able to do something. Maybe at Albert Einstein. Endless questions churned around in my mind. But one thought that managed to creep in more and more often was the thought that maybe, just maybe, something could be done. And if not, I hadn't really lost anything. I knew that we had to go and find out.

Einstein was different from any place that I had stayed. The doctors talked with a hint of optimism. They spoke openly of a possible bone chip in the fourth vertebra. If they could remove it, I might get additional return in my limbs. They talked of the possibility of braces for my legs.

I had a large, semi-private room. My schedule was typed out and given to me. It included every test that I could think of: X rays, muscle evaluation, occupational therapy evaluation, bowel and bladder evaluation, a myelogram, wheelchair evaluation, and brace evaluation. They wasted no time. On my second day there, I started twenty-one days of consecutive, thorough testing of every part of my body.

From the beginning, the tests challenged me. A nurse, a therapist, or a doctor was always with me, encouraging me to hang on, to be a little more patient, to undergo just one more test that day. I fought the weariness and put forth all the strength I could find for the evaluations. I wanted to show them how much I could do.

My final evaluation at Einstein was with leg braces. It was a new experience. A therapist and an attendant strapped my legs and lower back into a complicated brace of metal and pads. As they worked with the brace, I looked up at the parallel bars. I knew I would be carried to them in the next few minutes.

This, I thought, is what I had first thought rehabilitation was all about. Someone would stand me on my feet. Once up, my legs would take over. I would begin to shuffle my feet. I knew I would be slow and clumsy at first. Then I would take small steps. Finally, I would begin to walk.

That thinking had been changed by my stay at Fishersville. No matter, I had in front of me my first opportunity to stand since the accident.

I listened to the therapist as she told me what was going to happen and what she wanted me to do.

My heart beat harder as I thought about standing up.

The attendant locked his arms around my chest and lifted me to the bars. The therapist kneeled down and locked the braces at my knees. I looked at myself in the large wall mirrors in front. I was standing. But the image I saw in the mirrors sickened me. One of my feet turned in. My shoulders were pushed up above my neck as I pushed against the bars. The braces were the worst part. They were big and clumsy looking, hiding my legs. I looked like a cripple.

The attendant backed away. So did the therapist. I was now on my own.

"All right, Skip. Lock your arms at the elbows. And lift with your shoulder muscles. You want to try to raise your feet off the floor."

I tried to follow the therapist's instructions, but I couldn't. I pushed against the bars as hard as I could for a few seconds. What little strength I had in my arms and shoulders was gone. I had just barely lifted my feet. The effort drained me. I nearly passed out. I was carried back to the chair.

I sat exhausted, staring into the wall mirrors and thinking about what had happened. My arms and shoulders ached. My body throbbed out the message of how difficult the brief test had been.

There would be no more attempts. The test was over and I wasn't going to walk or even stand. The guarded hope that I had brought to Albert Einstein flowed out of me as I sat in that chair. I had looked like a cripple in front of the mirrors. I began to accept the fact that I was crippled.

Still weak from the efforts at the bars, I began to suffer ill effects from an earlier myelogram as I sat with Mom and Dad.

The doctor was summing up the long days of testing.

"We have been unable to find a bone chip. There isn't anything else we can do here for Skip. But the results are encouraging. His attitude is excellent. He can physically do more than we would expect for a person with his type of injury. It is possible, with surgery, that he can gain additional use of his hands.

The doctor continued to paraphrase for us the test results that were on the desk in front of him. I heard only words and partial sentences, but I knew what he was saying:

"Continue life as he is now . . . handicapped in a normal world."

His message was clear and he spoke it with courteous and sensitive finality.

"Go home. Prepare for the future. Start school immediately."

At home a few days later, after I had recovered from the myelogram, Dad dropped a bombshell at dinner.

"Skip, you know your mom and I have been checking on college for you. I think we ought to do exactly what the doctors suggested. We ought to start right away."

I started to say something, but he continued.

"I've checked into colleges around here and there is one that I think will meet our needs. It's a small one over in Chesapeake. Chesapeake Junior College. All of the classrooms are on one floor. The dean of students, his name is Thomas Russ, said that he would be happy to have you as a student. He wants to meet with us as soon as he can. Classes start in eleven days. I have an appointment for us tomorrow."

Now he stopped. He could see that I wanted to speak.

"Dad, that sounds great. But maybe we ought to wait a little while. Until I'm stronger. The second semester would be better, don't you think? It wouldn't be as hot and I'll be even better adjusted."

I knew Dad disliked the role he sometimes had to play in my life. He was the heavy, the unpopular messenger of the unpopular things that had to be done. But he played the role anyway.

"Skip," he said, "we've got college *now*. We're here together and we're all going to help. We've got to do it."

The girls chimed in, as if on cue.

"I'll be able to take you in the mornings before I go to school," Linda said.

Shirley and Karen promised to help me with my assignments, doing whatever writing and typing I would need.

There was no further discussion. My apprehensions remained, but, as I had nearly always done, I would follow my dad's advice.

10

School Days, School Days

Football was on my mind as Mom, Dad and I drove the five miles to Chesapeake Junior College for pre-registration. Before the accident, college had been important to me because of football. Athletics were out of the question now; college held the unpleasant promise of only books and classes. Chesapeake didn't even have a football team.

I began to acknowledge how important this step was to my future. I wondered whether or not I could succeed in the classroom. Studies had been unimportant to me in high school; I had lived for football and track.

As we pulled to a stop in front of the campus, I was shocked. It was small. It looked more like a house on a big lot. One building, one floor.

Dean Russ changed my disappointment. He was cordial to us and very proud of his college. I found myself caught up in being a college student. When he had finished going down the list of possible degrees, I kept thinking about one that he had mentioned early in his conversation: counseling. I had seen so many people helping others in the past year. Perhaps that was what I could do and do well.

I enthusiastically explained that I thought a career in counseling, particularly involving young people, was the proper choice. By the time I finished explaining my choice, Mom, Dad, and Dean Russ agreed with me.

That night, alone, I thought more carefully about what had

happened during the day. Events had moved faster than I could keep up with them. My earlier enthusiasm about a counseling career now gave way to the immediate future: getting around to classes; no friends; no study habits. That night before I fell asleep, I kept telling myself that I couldn't let anyone down, least of all myself.

I was scared as Mom came to a stop in the college parking lot on my first day of classes. The lot was crowded, people were everywhere and the campus now looked large and foreboding. Nervously I transferred to the wheelchair, conscious that several students glanced my way, then looked away when they saw me looking at them. It was an awkward beginning.

Small ramps had been placed at each doorway to the building. I was the only wheelchair student at the college. They had been built for me, by direction of Dean Russ.

Mom's good-bye was brief.

"I'll be here to pick you up at noon. And, Skippy, I'll pray for you." With that blessing, I was on my own as a college student.

I felt self-conscious in class. Other students took down pages of notes as the instructor lectured. I couldn't write. I was relieved when the class was dismissed early, but even more relieved when the instructor came to me with an assuring smile. He discussed my special needs, including the use of someone's notes and taking exams on an electric typewriter. He made my first day a little easier.

A student met me as I neared the door to leave the building at the end of classes.

"Can I give you a hand?" he asked.

"I sure would appreciate it. The ramps are a little steep for me." He smiled and helped me out.

I made my way down the sidewalk that surrounded the school. The students now spoke easily and naturally to me. Their casual friendliness helped more than they knew.

Mom drove me home. I was tired, mentally and physically; but I felt good about myself and my first day at college. I had made it through on my own.

That fall Dad and I knew it was time. We went back to the football stadium at Princess Anne to see a ball game.

When we pulled into the parking lot, I suddenly was back in school as a student. A Friday night in the fall. I could hear the cleats scraping along the parking lot as I saw myself walk with the team from the dressing room to the edge of the field.

I hardly heard what Dad said to me as he pushed me toward the end zone. People stopped us along the way. They spoke to me, told me how glad they were to see me, and told me how much they'd enjoyed watching me play.

It was a haunting feeling. I sat near the end zone and looked onto the field bathed in floodlights. Memories of my runs and touchdowns on that field came flooding back. A sadness that I hadn't experienced for a long time returned.

I wondered what might have happened if there had been no accident.

Someone stopped to speak and interrupted my thoughts. As he left us, the familiar drumroll began. I instinctively looked to the goalposts. I knew the team would be lining up there to run onto the field for pregame calisthenics. They were there. I knew what was going through their minds. I had felt the nervousness that came before each game. And it never disappeared until the first play was called, the first contact made.

The drumroll gave way to the sound of the full band playing. The team sprinted between the goalposts and onto the field. Some of the players looked my way. There were a couple of waves and a couple of "thumbs up" signs in my direction.

Even if the lights had been better, I wouldn't have known who the players were. My eyes were full of tears.

While my return to the football field had a deep emotional impact on me, my return to my church had very little impact at all.

Except for my one brief try at praying and reading God's Word in the early days at Fishersville, I had been without any spiritual influence or interest.

Now the influence was present, but the interest remained absent. I attended church with the family. I continued to believe in God; he had been a major part of my upbringing. But I didn't have a personal relationship with him. I knew that he was out there somewhere, perhaps looking down on me. But that's about as much thought as I gave it.

Actually, church became more of a hindrance than a help. Whenever people at church would come up to me and claim that my courage and my determination made me a fine example of one of God's people, I recoiled with a sense of dishonesty. I became annoyed, even angry at the number of people who came to me to share stories about friends and relatives who suffered similar accidents and recovered through prayer and God's healing. I didn't know what God had in store for me, but I couldn't see how he was going to heal me. All I knew was what I had heard over and over: Prepare for a future life, Skip, with what you have now.

I tried, whenever I could and with whatever excuses I could find, to avoid a religious life altogether. But I tried just as hard not to let Mom and Dad know my feelings. That, I felt, would have been the biggest blow to them since the accident. Especially to Mom.

Mom, more than anyone else in the family, had enough burdens now that I was home. She was the primary caretaker for all of my needs.

The strains that the accident, my rehabilitation, and present condition had brought into the house showed from time to time. Tempers would flare, sometimes over the smallest things. One morning I lashed out at Mom simply because the cuff to my pants leg had become twisted, showing the top of my sock. She hadn't straightened it and I couldn't. But we were quick to forgive and we wouldn't allow anyone to brood over problems. As a family, we fought the tension and we tried to drive it out of the house as soon as it surfaced.

It helped that I was beginning to make friends at school. I went to keg parties and drank my first beers. I'd never wanted alcohol before. It had never been in our home. It wasn't even discussed. But almost everybody in college drank and I tried it out of self-consciousness and a need to be accepted. The thought of what was waiting for me at home after my first drink, if either Mom or Dad detected beer on my breath, made me stop for chewing gum before the night was over. It wasn't long before I stopped drinking.

I also began to have a social life at home, thanks to Dad. He bought a pool table for me. It was another example of how much he cared about me. The garage was his special place, the place where he went to be alone and to tinker. After we picked out the pool table, he cleared his tools and his projects from the garage and set up the table. The garage soon became a special place for me and for a growing number of friends.

There was a girl in my life, too—Martha Chevalier. Throughout 1968, the year that I returned home, Martha became the most important person in my life. Despite the fact that we had dated when I had received so much attention as an athlete, she accepted me now as I was.

I worried about not being able to take her out easily. But she assured me constantly that those things didn't matter, that she was happy just being with me, whether it was helping me with schoolwork or being out with others. I was still trying to fully accept my disability and wasn't always persuaded by what she said. I often picked arguments with her about trivial things and expressed doubt about her feelings for me just to see what she would say. I tested her affection continually, even in the face of all she did for me and all she meant to me.

There were times when physical feelings, as well as emotional ones, seemed very natural. On those occasions I allowed myself to think about Martha being a part of my life forever.

In January a member of the Cosmopolitan Club of Norfolk paid us a visit. R. E. Dorer explained that his organization undertook an annual project to provide help to an average family which suddenly found that it needed assistance. The club was interested in finding out whether I had some need that it could help fill. Dad told him about the practical need to enlarge my room to provide study space.

Mr. Dorer then spent some time talking alone with me. He wanted to know about my plans for the future. Then he asked me to outline my ideas for a complete room of my own.

He left, saying he would be back in touch.

Several weeks later he returned. The Cosmopolitan Club wanted to build an addition to the house. Not only would I have my own entrance and ample space to study, but I was to have a roll-in shower. No longer would Mom and Dad have to carry me from my chair, through the narrow hallway and into the tub. Construction would begin as soon as we could provide the plans. By November the work was completed and I had gained another measure of independence.

That summer, in 1969, our place in North Carolina lured me back. It had represented fun and shared moments of happiness with the family—until the accident.

My first trip back, the summer before, had been painful. I sat looking over the waters where I had skied, run the boat, and fished. That day, all I could think about was a future without those things that I'd enjoyed so much. On a later visit with Martha that summer, Uncle Ackie and Dad rigged a lawn chair in the boat for me and I went cruising with them on the Sound. It whetted my appetite for the water.

Now Bill Milleson, a friend in college, helped change those year-old feelings of frustration about not being able to go boating. He had lost interest in a small haul-seine boat that he was building and he had offered to finish it for my possible use.

I was excited. I approached Dad about the idea and he took it instantly.

Bill and Dad got some help on the project from two friends who put in flooring and rigged a steering system. A 10-horsepower motor was the finishing touch. The four of them mounted a crane on the side of the dock with an old boat winch to lower me aboard, seated in the wheelchair, and lift me out.

As I was lowered into the completed boat on a beautiful summer day, I realized how fortunate I was to have a family and friends who worked so hard for a gift that meant so much to me.

The boat opened another freedom for me—I could once again control myself on the Sound. It brought back to all of us a sense of happiness about Carolina.

The return to Carolina also toppled a psychological barrier for the family. Dad had lost interest in boating after the accident. He was especially reluctant to take the girls waterskiing. Not only did it remind him of the accident, but he also felt that if I saw the girls on skis, I would always be reminded of what had happened to my life.

Now, I was the one who knew the time had come. Linda and I bought a slalom ski. We gave it to Dad one night after dinner and told him it was for Karen and Shirley. He didn't say anything, but he looked at me for a long time. I knew that he was asking me if I could handle the image of one of my sisters on the thing that had crippled me. I nodded to him. The single ski reopened a world that had been shut to all of us. That summer became one of the happiest that I ever had. I felt that, in some small way, I had given something to the family that had given so much to me.

In the fall Martha returned to Longwood College for her second year. We began to develop different sets of friends and activities and interests. Our letters became less and less frequent. I began to push her out of my life. On the few occasions that we saw each other, our relationship was definitely different. I wasn't confident enough to believe that we could make it together and I didn't want to cause her unhappiness in the future.

We saw each other for the last time as a couple during the Christmas holidays. It was difficult for both of us. She meant so much to me, yet I believed that I was doing the right thing—for her sake and for mine. I missed her the moment she left our house on the last day that we saw each other. Maybe one day in the future I would be able to accept love, like Martha's, that was given without concern for my condition. But I couldn't now.

The sadness over Martha was countered by a joyful Christmas

morning. After the family had opened presents at home, we drove to Granny's and Papa's. The visit was both a family reunion and a Christmas celebration. Auntie and Uncle Ackie were present for my first traditional Christmas breakfast since the accident. Conversation and laughter filled the house from the moment we arrived until we left that afternoon.

The trip to Granny's was only twelve miles, but as I thought back on our somber Christmas of 1967, I realized that all of us had traveled closer to becoming a whole family once again.

I was soon to realize just how valuable my family's love and support were to me.

When I returned to college for the second semester, a nightmare greeted me. Over the holidays, the quadriplegic who had enrolled in the fall had taken his own life.

He and I had been similar in some ways. We had about the same degree of physical limitations. Both of us were tackling college head-on, maneuvering around or rolling right over the small problems that cropped up.

There were differences, too. His parents had provided for him in a way that my parents couldn't. He had a specially equipped car. He had his own home that had been customized for his handicaps. He had a small swimming pool in the yard. I must have had the one thing that he needed—the desire to keep on living. For many days after learning of his death, I thought back thankfully to the discipline, to the emotional strengthening that I had received at the hands of Dr. O'Hanlan at Fishersville. I thought about my parents who had given me their bedroom, about Dad who had given up his private place in the garage. My whole family had given themselves to me, helping me to find courage when I lost it and to keep my determination close at hand.

I thought how tragic it must have been for my schoolmate. To have had so much and yet not enough. I knew that his parents, who had tried so hard, must have felt pain and frustration. My heart went out especially to his sister, no older than my own sister Karen. She had found her brother, and the shotgun and the yardstick that he had used to reach down from his wheelchair to trip the trigger to end his life.

I vowed, no matter what happened in my future, that I would never put my family through such an ordeal. Out of this almost unspeakable tragedy, I found one more reason to keep on going.

11

Daphne

I was at a party one night and a tall, slim, dark-haired young lady walked by me. So I did what any normal, healthy twenty-year-old would do—I had my sister go check her out!

Daphne Via: outgoing, attractive, two years younger than me, graduate of Princess Anne. Linda reported back to me all the important information, including the fact that Daphne had agreed to accept a date with me if I asked her for one.

"Skip," Linda said, "it's set. All you have to do is call her."

I went home and called Daphne. Well, I called her about five months later. After all, I didn't want to move too quickly. . . .

A Friday night school dance. That seemed like a relatively safe first date. But I hadn't quite bargained for how it would turn out.

Don Pollard was driving his van. He, Rob McClintoch, and I were headed for the dance. Their dates had fallen through at the last minute and I was embarrassed about taking Daphne without any other girls. But there was no turning back.

We stopped for beer and then for Daphne.

Don went to the door. As I watched him go up the walkway, I felt insecure that I couldn't call for her and meet her parents. I realized how nervous I was.

As I was worrying about all of the things that I wanted to do and couldn't, Daphne appeared at the door of the van.

"Hi, Daphne, I'm sorry that I couldn't . . ."

"Don't worry about it. I understand," she said. She smiled and climbed in and we quickly fell into a conversation about mutual friends, days at Princess Anne, and what we now were doing. She was instantly easy to be with and a lot of fun. We enjoyed the dance, talking and joking almost nonstop. The four of us decided to ride to the beach after the dance. Don and Rob went off to one of our favorite spots to drink beer and Daphne and I continued our conversation alone in the van.

She was sitting on the backseat of the van and I asked if she would like for me to join her. When she said yes, I began to transfer from the chair to the seat, something I hadn't done before in a van. She amazed me. She held the chair and offered assistance, easily, without fumbling and without awkwardness.

All I could think about as we continued to talk was how much I wanted to kiss her. She was so pretty and so comfortable to be with. I knew, after only a few hours, that I liked her very much and that I wanted to see her again.

My desire to kiss her was slowed by questions that I hadn't asked myself since the accident, despite other dates.

I wondered how she'd react, whether I would make some awkward move and be embarrassed. For some reason, it was very important that Daphne Via be impressed with me.

But the desire finally won out. I had to try.

I leaned toward her and she leaned to meet me. It was a gentle kiss. My arms were around her and I held her for just a moment before it ended.

Shortly after my date with Daphne, I went to a Princess Anne basketball game. Karen was a cheerleader and I was beginning to follow her career at home games just the way she had followed my football games and track meets.

During halftime, a man came over and introduced himself.

"Skip. I'm Larry Via."

I was taken by surprise. When he realized that I was confused, he said in a bold, clipped way, "I'm Daphne's dad. You dated my daughter last weekend. Remember?"

Before I could answer, he went on.

"She had some nice things to say about you. I've read about you, too. If there's anything I can ever do for you, you just let me know, you hear? And come back to see Daphne soon. And meet the rest of her family."

I was overwhelmed. On the next date, Daphne brought her mom, Helen, and her dad out to the van to meet me formally. They made me feel comfortable in spite of the fact that they had to come to the van to meet me.

Several weeks later, I was invited to a Sunday supper at the Vias. Daphne picked me up in her family's station wagon. Mr. Via came to the door to lift the chair up the steps to the front porch.

"Skip, we're going to have to build a ramp for you," he said matter-of-factly.

When I rode with Daphne to her house for my next visit, there was a ramp going up to the front porch.

"Daph, that's really nice of your dad." That was all I could say. I wanted to say much more. The ramp meant to me that the Vias accepted me, wheelchair and all.

My life became a busy combination of attending class and dating Daphne.

College broadened into an active social life. New friends visited, shot pool, and stayed at the house in the evenings to talk, watch television, or listen to records. Occasionally we played poker until late into the night. Friends would often be invited to stay for dinner. Life was similar to my high school days. In the early days of my return home, I remembered what Robert Smith and Dr. O'Hanlan had told me when I left Fishersville. They had been right. Many of my old friends had gone on with their lives while I was away. I had to accept myself and form new friendships with people who would take me as I was.

Daphne and I saw each other several times a week. We double-dated almost all of the time because of the transportation difficulties. Don Pollard and another classmate, Nancy Schmidt, became close friends and we spent much of our time with them.

Mary and Paul Bradley became very important to Daphne and me. I had met Paul at our place in Carolina when I was six. His parents lived in Norfolk and had a summer place near ours. Paul was older than I, but during the summer he would take me on hunting and fishing trips and let me run with him as he worked out. As I matured, he and his wife became my close friends. I wanted very much for the Bradleys to like Daphne.

Paul, Mary, and their four children lived near Norfolk's DePaul School of Nursing where Daphne was enrolled. Paul would pick Daphne up after her classes, I would get a ride to the Bradley's, and the four of us would fix dinner together and enjoy the evening.

Now that I was dating steadily, money became a problem. Since the accident, Mom and Dad always made sure that I had spending money. My grandparents frequently helped. But my need had increased and I was embarrassed about having to ask each time I dated.

Mom became my sounding board to solve the problem. She knew, but never said, that my feelings for Daphne were becoming stronger. As it always happened, Mom passed my concerns to Dad. That night he helped me solve the problem.

"Skip, I'm going to give you fifteen dollars a month from now on. But I know that you'll have special things come up for you and Daphne. And there're going to be times when something unexpected happens. I want you to come to me when that happens and I'll try to help you out."

Papa and Granny also began to give me a monthly amount. The allotments weren't large, but Daphne and I found enjoyment in planning together what we could do with the money.

Daphne and I weren't uncomfortable about my condition. After our first date, we talked frequently about my limitations and needs as we planned to go to parties or to be with friends.

Daphne had learned about some of my physical problems and requirements in her nursing classes; others came up in our conversations; and still others became a part of what linked us together as a couple rather than separating us.

I had become accustomed to the sheath and the leg bag, but I was sensitive about them around Daphne.

Often when we were out with friends, I would excuse myself to go outside to empty the bag, always asking one of my male friends to accompany me. I was unable to bend down far enough or pull my leg up high enough to unclamp the drainage tube at the bottom of the bag. Daphne insisted that she could help me, that there was no need for me to be sensitive about it.

One evening, when I needed to excuse myself from the table where we were talking, she followed the two of us outside.

"Skip, I can help you with that," she said.

I turned to Don. "OK, Don. We'll be in in a minute."

Daphne easily unclamped the tube to drain the bag, straightened my pant leg, and pushed me back inside as if she had performed the task hundreds of times.

Daphne fit into my life more and more easily. On the weekends in May of 1970, she went with Mom and the girls to clean the trailer for our summer months in Currituck Sound. She came back with a deeper understanding of why Carolina was so special to me. And she came back having begun a closer friendship with Linda. I felt a real joy as I watched the two of them growing to care about each other more and more.

That summer on Currituck Sound brought me another kind of joy, too.

Bass fishing had always meant a freedom, a serenity, and a competition that bound men together. I could not remember a summer before the accident that I had not had a bass rod in my hand. Now, with no grip in my hands, I couldn't hold, let alone handle a bass rod.

Watson Stuart, a summertime friend at Carolina, and Paul Bradley helped me take up fishing again. It wasn't bass that we were after; it was white perch.

Even with the limited ability in my hands, I could cradle the pole loosely in both palms. Because the cane pole had no flexibility, as a bass rod did, and no reel, I was able to lean back and jerk the pole to hook perch. Watson or Paul would set the proper length of line and set the bobber at the right height for the depth of water we happened to be fishing in.

Sometimes we would drop anchor; other times just drift in the boat.

When we decided on a spot, those of us in the boat—sometimes two, sometimes three of us—would beat the water rapidly with the poles to imitate the sound of schools of minnows rushing through the water. White perch are one of the few fish that are attracted and not frightened by sound. Within minutes, one of us would feel the first fish hit the hook.

From then on, if the school of perch had followed the lead fish, we'd hook and jerk the catch into the boat. We sometimes caught as many as fifty fish in ten minutes. Often Daphne went with me. She became adept at taking fish off my hook so I could return my line quickly to the water. Mom taught her how to clean the fish.

I'd had a full day on the water on June 26, a Friday. Daphne had arrived at Carolina that afternoon and we were happy because she had finished her nurses' classes for the semester. She had a job in the emergency room at General Hospital of Virginia Beach. Most of the summer still stretched ahead of us.

The family had settled for the night. As was our custom, Daphne and I were resting on my bed in the living room of the trailer. I was dressed for bed and under the bedcovers. She was propped up next to me, lounging on top of the covers. The moon was full and it beamed through the large window that overlooked Currituck Sound. There was a sparkling pathway of light across the water.

"Daph," I said. The words came out softly. "Could you see yourself spending the rest of your life with me?"

There was a brief silence, then she slowly propped herself on one elbow and looked down at me.

"Are you asking me to marry you?"

"If you think that we can make it, I'd like to give it a go."

Tears came to her eyes. We held each other for a long time.

"I don't know when I can get you a ring," I said. "I don't even know when we can get married. You have school to finish and so do I. I don't even know if I can get a job when I finish school.

"You know we'll have a different kind of physical love than other couples, and I have no idea about children. But I know that I love you and that you're the person I'd like to live the rest of my life with."

Never in my life had I felt so good about anything. Daphne Via, beautiful and bright, full of life and love, was excited about becoming my wife.

I broke the gentle quiet that had fallen over us.

"Daphne, can't you just see it?" I said in the same soft and thoughtful voice.

"We'll be married here at Carolina. Maybe on the pier. We can have the guys holding pole canes. That's it. We'll walk under an arch of pole canes."

Daphne poked me playfully.

"I don't care," she said, "when or where or how. I just know that I want to marry you, Skip Wilkins."

12

Among the Goals

The pleasurable days of summer slowly gave way to fall.

I was eager for classes to begin. I was in my final year at Chesapeake Junior College and I felt confident that I would be ready to transfer to a four-year college and get a full degree.

I rarely thought about my confinement to a wheelchair now. There were other things to occupy my mind. I had friends, good grades, and a growing sense of my own worth. I had been elected vice president of the student body earlier in the year. It hadn't been a tough campaign; we had no competition. But Bill Milleson, who ran for president, and I did generate some excitement and some enthusiasm for the school.

Our biggest and most successful campaign ploy took place the night before election day. The college had no flagpole on campus. Bill had salvaged a twenty-five-foot pole used to hold fish nets in Chesapeake Bay. We gathered together some of our "campaign staff"—we had enlisted the aid of all of our friends at school, assuring a victory even if we had had competition—and spent the midnight hours installing the pole in front of the main entrance. I didn't give a second thought to the fact that I was wheeling around in the dark, giving directions and providing encouragement to a dozen classmates; I did acknowledge to myself that I was thoroughly enjoying the escapade.

Once the pole was in place, we hoisted an American flag. The next morning the flag waved in a steady breeze as students arrived. Low on the pole we had attached a painted sign, "Contributed by the Milleson and Wilkins Campaign." The flag, to the delight of the students, flew daily the rest of the school year.

I concentrated on my studies and my life. Daphne and I spent all of our free time together. We continued to be frequent guests in the Bradley household and at our favorite spots at the beach. Whenever I went out socially, I went with Daphne.

Though it seems impossible, I was feeling contentment in the face of permanently limited physical life.

But my contentment and the serenity that had settled over life in our home was suddenly shattered on Sunday evening, January 17, 1971.

I was lying alone in my room. For no apparent reason, I felt very tired and weak. The cause of my fatigue became apparent about 6:00 P.M. when Mom started to drain my leg bag. There was no mistaking what I saw. I had blood particles in my urine, an abnormal and frightening development.

I soon became nauseated. I knew that whatever was wrong was serious; my body was sending me that message with the vomiting, the splotches of sweat, the chills, and the aching.

Dad measured the amount of fluid that I had been able to pass during the evening; three pints. Three pints out of five quarts of water that I had had. He was worried and so was I. I called Daphne to tell her that I was leaving for Norfolk General, that she shouldn't worry, and that I didn't think it was anything serious. But I really needed for her to tell me to be calm and not worry.

Dr. Poutasse wasn't available, but his intern was. I was in excruciating pain by the time I reached the emergency room. I vomited again. My bladder continued to distend and I could get no relief. I simply couldn't void. I was almost glad when the doctor said that he was going to insert a catheter to enable me to void and to relieve the pressure building up in my bladder. I was in so much pain that the psychological fear of the catheter didn't come.

My bladder emptied. I felt as though I had just finished the hardest-hitting football game of my life. My upper chest, my shoulders, my neck, my head, and my arms ached.

The doctor said I could return home. Both Dad and I were worried. We didn't know what had caused the problem and we didn't know whether it would return. The doctor tried to assure us that he didn't believe that it was serious.

As I lay awake that night, I knew something was definitely wrong. I could sense it. As if to endorse my fear, my body heaved and contracted and I vomited again. Only this time nothing came out. I hadn't eaten since lunch. I exhausted myself wondering what the next day would bring and I fell asleep.

I awoke without the chills and fever that I had experienced the night before. I was able to void. I tried to eat, but couldn't. It was difficult to force liquids down. *The problem, whatever it is, is still there,* I thought.

By 10:00 A.M. Monday the chills returned. I tried to force more liquids, hoping it would ease the problem. My temperature began to climb—by 1:00 P.M. I was on my way to the hospital again.

The examination in the emergency room was long and extensive. Intravenous pyelograms (IVPs) were taken and I was put on intravenous liquids and given antibiotics.

By early Monday evening my temperature had stabilized at 101 degrees. After several more hours of observation and no reduction in the fever, I was admitted to Intensive Care. It was 10:00 P.M. I was exhausted, frightened, and sick. My surroundings added to my fear. I was back in the place where it had all begun less than four years earlier.

I tried to eat the next morning, but I couldn't keep anything down. My heartbeat was rapid. I had never experienced any problems with my heart and I was scared. With each beat, I thought my heart would explode and burst through my chest. It was as though someone were inside pounding against my chest with a sledge. Soon, a throbbing headache accompanied the pounding of my heart. The harder my heart beat, the more frightened I became and the stronger the poundings became.

A specialist in internal medicine was called. Each minute added confusion. I underwent more X rays, then an EKG. I began vomiting again although there was nothing in my stomach to empty. I was catheterized again and the pounding and the pressure in my head and heart lessened for a short while. I returned to a private room.

Tuesday night a private nurse came to stay with me. I was too weak to ask why she was there.

The next three days and nights seemed endless. I was barely aware of the visits by Mom, Dad, and Daphne. I still had blood in my urine and my heart and head had not stopped the constant and fearful pounding. The doctors finally isolated the potential problem. They performed a cystoscopy and found infection in my bladder. They changed my medications and ordered stronger sedatives to provide some relief from the constant pains in my head and upper body.

Slowly I began to respond. Dr. Poutasse was now treating me. I felt secure in his care because he had helped me so much before.

Two more days passed and the problems diminished. On Sunday, one week after the problem had begun, Dr. Poutasse released me and instructed Dad to bring me back to the hospital at the first sign of any problem.

I was home for three days. On Thursday, the chills returned with the fever, the nausea, and the aching. By 7:00 P.M. that night I was back in the emergency room, this time rushed there by the rescue squad. As I lay in the back of the vehicle with its red lights flashing and the siren wailing as we approached an intersection, I thought back to my ambulance ride in June of 1967. I had felt then that I was going to die. Once again, I felt that I was close to death.

My temperature registered 105 degrees when I was admitted to Intensive Care. I was given antibiotics and put on an ice mattress. For the next three days, medicine and constant supervision of my vital signs were my whole life.

Once again the fever began to drop. Finally it returned to normal. After five more days in the hospital, I was well enough to be sent home. I stayed at home for two days, then tried to return to school. I couldn't make it. I was too weak. Professors sent assignments home and I tried doing the work in bed. Daphne visited as often as she could, but she had her own schoolwork. When she couldn't visit, she called and sent cards. Her visits and her messages bolstered me and I managed to hang onto some will to get better.

Late in the night of February 7, the chills and the fever came back. The next morning I was back in Intensive Care.

I had first become sick on January 17. It was now February 8. I had been taken to the hospital four times in twenty-three days. I was in Intensive Care for the third time in three weeks. As I lay in bed that night, weak and afraid, I cried out to God.

"Why?" I asked him. "Why? Why now? When I've accepted my accident. Why are these things happening to me? Why more problems?"

I had never called out to him before, but I was scared and I was desperate. I couldn't understand why I was being punished again. What had I done to deserve this sickness and this pain? Only God, as I understood him, could do this. *Surely,* I thought, *he must have a reason.*

Three days and nights passed with no improvement. I was growing steadily weaker. There had been other times that I had been depressed and I had somehow managed to work my way back to a positive attitude. But now I had nothing left to fight with. I was so tired. I felt defeated, mentally and physically. The fever continued. I had constant and severe chest pains. My heart and my head increased their pounding each time my bladder tried to drain, even with the use of the catheter.

Mom was sitting next to me by the bed that night. I think she knew that I was ready to give up.

"Mom," I said, "I don't know if we're going to make it this time."

When my words came out, we both felt fear. It was the first

time that I had ever admitted the possibility of death.

She reached for my hand.

"Skippy, you *are* going to make it. Of course you are. We're with you. Your dad. And the girls. And me. We've come so far. All of us. And you have Daphne to live for. She cares so much for you."

Mom was giving me the last bit of strength that she had saved for herself. Usually it was Dad who exhorted and encouraged, not allowing me to give up. Now here was Mom, talking so quietly and giving me reason and resolve to keep fighting when I was at my lowest point.

Tears came and so did some last, small measure of strength.

It was enough.

Three days had passed since I had been brought back to the hospital. Dr. Poutasse was standing over me.

"Skip, I think we've found the cause of your problems. Your bladder, since our first operation, has grown back some of that muscle. It can't empty completely.

"It's been continuing to hold some urine. Residual, we call it. And that residual has been creating serious infection. The antibiotics have been able to clear the infection each time we've used them, but they haven't eliminated the problem. We need to perform another resection. I've got to clip away some of that muscle that's grown back. You'll be on special medications from now on to prevent infection. But I think that will take care of it."

I never thought that I would be excited at the prospect of another operation, but I was. For the first time in nearly a month there appeared to be an answer. Something could be done to end the sickness.

I wondered to myself, when Dr. Poutasse left, *Could God have heard my cry to him three days ago and allowed this answer to come?*

I really wasn't sure, but for the first time in my life I felt that maybe God had answered me. In the only way that I knew how— quietly and alone—I thanked him.

I was operated on the next morning. The second transurethral resection was simple and fast. Dr. Poutasse cut away a little more muscle at the neck of my bladder. Once again, it began to function properly.

While I was recuperating in the hospital, I bought an engagement ring.

One of my college friends dropped by to visit. He began telling me about breaking up with his fiancée. She had given the ring back to him. As he poured out his sorrows and fingered the ring absentmindedly in his hands, he looked out the window toward the Elizabeth River.

"Skip, you know what I'm going to do when I leave here? I'm going to walk over to the river and toss this ring as far as I can."

I instantly thought how much I would like to have a ring for Daphne, but I knew that my finances wouldn't allow that for a long time to come.

"Hey, Larry, you can't do that. That thing cost a lot of money. I wish I had a ring. . . ."

He looked up. "Here, you want this one? You can have it. I sure don't need it anymore."

"No," I said, "I couldn't do that." But I did become excited about the prospect.

"Here, take it." He shoved it toward me.

"No, I couldn't take it. What would Daphne think if she found out that I gave her a ring that somebody had just *given* to me?" I kept looking at that ring and thinking about Daphne.

He sensed that I wasn't going to accept it as a gift.

"OK. Give me five bucks for it."

"Sold," I said.

I reached for my wallet, gave him five dollars, and put the ring away. I didn't know when I would use it, but I definitely knew who was going to wear it.

I regained my strength, but remained in Norfolk General for another operation. This one was scheduled for my hand.

Dad had followed up on the Albert Einstein test findings on my hands; there was a possibility for improved use of my fingers.

Before the bladder infection had sidetracked my life, I had visited with Dr. Jerome Adamson, a plastic surgeon in Norfolk.

I had no finger control in either hand. The little finger of my right hand was permanently extended, making it a constant and easy victim of cuts, scrapes and other damage. My other three fingers and thumb on my right hand were paralyzed in a folded position inside my palm. The fingers on my left hand also were folded into my palm. The best I could do was to use both hands as paws to pick up objects between them.

Based on examination and tests, Dr. Adamson believed that a successful tendon transplant could give me greater use of my fingers and hands. The transplant might provide some gripping ability to allow me to do things I could not do now. He decided to operate first on my right hand because it was stronger and had more potential than the left.

He explained that the surgery would be extremely long and complicated. Having fought the bladder problem, I was open to anything that might bring more improvement. I envisioned a normal hand after Dr. Adamson completed the operation, even though he cautioned me that that was not possible.

As I gradually moved from the darkness and sleep of the anesthetic in surgery into the light of my hospital room, I felt pain in my right arm. It was such a deep pain that I tried futilely to stay under the control of the drug. I looked at my right arm. It was attached to an IV pole and extended upright in the air. A cast encased my lower arm, wrist, and fingers to their tips. The throbbing ache reminded me of pain I had felt in my chest and my head only days earlier.

Dr. Adamson explained that scores of stitches had been required to close the surgery and that my arm should remain elevated, morning and night, for six weeks to allow it to heal properly.

The six weeks of recuperation at home were difficult for all of us. I was now unable to do anything for myself. I was helpless again. We constantly cheered each other with talk of my being able to use my right hand.

When Dr. Adamson cut away the cast six weeks later, I looked at an ugly, misshapen, and severely shriveled arm. The smell of the dead flesh and the dried blood and the sight of the endless lines of stitches made me faint.

I foolishly had expected a normal-looking hand. I didn't have it. But as I began to strengthen the atrophied arm muscles with prescribed exercises and to work with the fingers, I found that I did have some finger movement.

After the first operation, Dr. Adamson recommended a second operation on the hand. The thumb was not in its proper position and needed a pin to stabilize it. The tendon controlling the little finger needed to be tightened, and I needed more tendon work to allow me to lift my hand at the wrist.

The second hand operation in June was scheduled for six and a half hours, but was cut short. Some of the surgical work could not be performed. But the same pain was there when I came out of the anesthetic. And the cast. And the need to keep the arm elevated for six weeks.

When the second cast was cut away, I had some finger control and, because my thumb had been stabilized, I had some grip in my right hand. The fingers were still contorted, but not as badly as before the two operations.

A third operation was needed to complete the repair to my right hand. Then the same kind of operations would be performed on the left hand and fingers.

I couldn't bring myself to agree. And no one in the family tried to change my mind. I had endured the awful pain of surgery twice. I had some use of my fingers. I was willing to learn to live with that limitation, but I wasn't willing to go through another operation on my hand.

A reporter, Beth Polson, called me in March for an interview. She was the writer for the "Lively Age" section of the afternoon newspaper, *The Ledger-Star*.

The interview went well. She was easy to talk to and she showed an interest in me and my life. When I saw the interview in the paper, I felt a sense of pride and fulfillment for the family; someone had recognized how hard we had fought to keep going and was giving all of us credit.

She had asked two questions that, until the interview, I had avoided. As I read her interview, I was aware of how much she had helped me by forcing me to think about and to answer the two questions.

"What," she had asked, "do you plan to do when you leave Chesapeake Junior College this spring? And what are your goals in life?"

I hadn't thought about my future in terms that specific. But when she had asked, I had to come to grips with answers that satisfied me.

Now I was reading what she had written:

"Everything to me is like a goal. I set small goals, then I set large goals."

Among the large goals is an ambition to be a guidance counselor. "I'd like to come back here (Chesapeake College) to teach some day," he said. A psychology major, he plans to transfer eventually to Virginia Wesleyan. "We're not able to yet; it's too expensive," he said.

Marriage is also among the goals. Right now he's dating a nursing student at DePaul Hospital.

"I want to be a success," he said, "and help others in any way."

As I thought about what I had said in the interview—finish college, get a job, and marry, I realized how badly I wanted to achieve those goals for myself, for Daphne, and for the family. I knew that completing college was necessary to a life of security and independence and we had talked about it at home. But my special needs and the expense of college had raised a question that we hadn't yet answered: where to go?

The newspaper story helped us find the answer.

Three days after the story appeared, Dad got a call from Al Roosendaal, the father of one of my old football teammates. He was a member of a local Lions Club and he had read the newspaper story. He wanted to know if we might be agreeable to accepting financial aid from the Lions, if there were a college nearby where I could finish my education.

Dad had me in the car the next day, heading to Virginia Wesleyan College for an appointment with the president, Lambuth M. Clarke. I had heard good things about Wesleyan, but I hadn't visited there.

My first reaction to the campus was one of disappointment. Before Dad had parked the car, I could see problems. There were no ramps. I knew that there had been at least one wheelchair student. I wondered how he had gotten around. Some of the buildings were two and three stories high. That meant stairways. Were there elevators? The questions mounted as I glanced around the campus.

President Clarke's conversation erased many of the concerns. The buildings did have elevators. The college would schedule as many of my classes as possible on the ground-floor level. There would be no problems about transferring my credits from Chesapeake. My grades, he said as he reviewed them, were very acceptable and I would enter Wesleyan as a junior.

The day after Mr. Roosendaal had received commitments from each of the Lions Clubs in the Virginia Beach area, he called Dad at home.

The Lions, he said, wanted to provide me with a scholarship to Virginia Wesleyan. It would cover, completely, tuition and books as long as I did my part and maintained a satisfactory grade point average.

Suddenly the absence of ramps at Wesleyan was of no conse-quence to me. We had been given a way to provide for my contin-ued education.

The gift from the Lions Club strengthened my belief that I could overcome whatever obstacles lay ahead. I wanted to finish school and I *was going to finish* school. That was the key to a job and a life with Daphne.

13

Be Prepared to Change

Our place at Currituck Sound became our true summer home in 1971. Dad acquired a larger trailer and put it on a foundation next to Granny and Papa's trailer. We had a growing number of guests. Karen was dating now and brought her friends to visit. The family spent every weekend there.

My hand healed, and my partial grip became stronger as I pushed myself through my exercises. I was driven in part by a secret hope that perhaps I could find some way to return to bass fishing. I often sat with Daphne on the lawn that bordered the Sound, watching bass fishermen heading out to work the grass beds and the shoreline.

Midway through the summer, on a warm, lazy Saturday afternoon, I held my fly rod in my hand for the first time in four years. Two friends, David Atkins and David Hopson, had helped me secure the rod in my right hand. We wrapped an elastic bandage around my open hand and fastened it at my wrist. I was able to slip the end of the rod between the bandage and my palm, using the new strength and flexibility in my fingers to steady the rod.

It felt comfortable and secure.

I began to try to cast the bug. I had little wrist movement and the first tries were awkward and unsuccessful. I kept at it and was able to control the rod well enough to cast the bug in the direction I wanted it to land. It wasn't graceful, but it was effective.

The three of us got into the boat and headed for a near shoreline. David Hopson got out to fish alone. David Atkins checked my rod and bug and then tied the bow line around his waist. He began wading along the shore, working his rod and slowly pulling the boat. I was able to cast and suddenly I was bass fishing again. We worked the shoreline all afternoon, finally giving up as darkness set in. I came home empty-handed, but I had improved my control over the rod and the bug.

My first bass since the accident came the next morning. It was small, not even a "keeper," but it represented another victory over my handicap. Landing the fish became a two-man job. When I felt the strike, I pulled back hard on the rod and hooked the fish, but I wasn't able to pull the line in with my left hand. I didn't have enough grip or strength. David came to the side of the boat and began taking up the slack in the line so I could play the fish with the rod. Slowly, as he continued to bring the line in, the bass came closer and closer to the boat. When it was beside the boat, I managed to grip the line and David raised the fish out of the water and into the boat. It didn't matter that the line had coiled around me and the chair. I had landed a bass.

As the summer neared its end, I was able to handle the line through my teeth and to play my fish without assistance.

I had found another reason to look forward to the future as we closed up the trailer for the winter. Bass fishing had become part of my life again.

Linda was married in the fall, just before I started at Virginia Wesleyan. I felt that I was losing touch with a very special person. In the spring, she had met Tom Viar, a student at the University of Virginia and one of the centers on the football team. They had dated steadily after their first meeting. I shared in her happiness but when she held me to say good-bye and to invite Daphne and me to visit her in Charlottesville, I felt that a large part of my life and my support was leaving. I realized how much she had done for me and just how much we loved each other.

Karen and her dates soon filled the void created by the departure of Linda and Tom. Shirley and I became closer and more attentive to each other now that we were frequently at home together.

My first day of classes at Wesleyan presented me with new problems. The college was much larger than Chesapeake Junior College and some of my classes had to be scheduled on the second floor.

I felt conspicuous as I pushed the button to the elevator to get to my second class of the day. I fumbled to get the key to the elevator into its slot. Nothing happened. I tried again and again. Still nothing happened. The elevator wasn't operating. I felt myself turning red with embarrassment as I realized that I was helpless and would be late for class on the first day. I wondered whether I would be able to handle this new environment.

My doubts ended as abruptly as they had started when a student offered to help. He stopped three others and the four of them lifted the chair and carried me up the stairs.

"I don't know how to thank you," I said as they put me down.

The student who had stopped to help me spoke.

"That's OK. There's a blind student here at Wesleyan, too. I help him out a lot in getting around and I read notes to him. If you need any more help, don't hesitate to ask. By the way, my name's Chuck Ratcliff."

I told him that I was uneasy about my first day at Wesleyan, I didn't know my way around, and it took me a long time to wheel from class to class—even if the elevators were working.

"Don't worry about it. I'll come back for you after this class and we'll get you where you need to go." With that, he turned and headed down the hall, leaving me with a feeling that I had found at least one student who understood some of my problems.

I had other adjustments to make. The first day of the second semester I was in a large class, larger than any I had ever attended. As I sat in the front of the room and students strolled in, chatting and kidding with each other, I again wondered if I could ever fit in at Wesleyan. It seemed so big and so impersonal.

The professor was late. When he came to the door, he announced in a terse voice that the class was being moved down the hall, that we were late starting, and that he expected everyone to move quickly to the new classroom.

Students began slapping their books in piles and shuffling out of the room.

I wanted to get started right away so I wouldn't be late, but I knew that I would cause a delay for the others. They filed out past me. There were no looks in my direction, no words spoken to me, and no offers of help.

When the room was empty, I started pushing toward the new class. It was a long and frustrating push. The hallway was carpeted, which added to the problem. I wasn't adept at pushing the chair rapidly, even with pegs on the rims. As I tried to go faster, my path became more and more erratic. It was a far cry from the run down the hall at Princess Anne, the day I started to run the hurdles.

A sense of anger at every student in the class began to build as I labored to get to the doorway where they had disappeared. The silence in the hallway was broken by the slamming of the classroom door. My anger grew into contempt. I didn't think anyone cared about me or my problems. There was no friendliness here, I thought. I had conveniently ignored Chuck's help, the help of other students and the assistance of professors up until now.

I was five minutes late getting into the classroom. The professor and the class glanced up as I tried to open the door and push in. Someone helped me with the door and everyone quickly returned their attention to the lecture.

The pain of being ignored became greater than my bitterness.

Why, I asked myself, *did no one help? What's wrong with them? What's wrong with me? How long is it going to be like this?*

I couldn't concentrate on the lecture going on in front of me. All during class, my mind kept repeating the questions. I tried to focus on the classwork, but it was futile.

I didn't get any answers to the questions. There was an answer, but I was too upset to remember it. Dr. O'Hanlan said it on the day I left Woodrow Wilson:

"Be prepared to change for the world. Because it won't change for you. It doesn't owe you anything."

The awkward, zigzag push down the hall that day taught me more about myself and what I would face than any course I had ever taken.

My requirements at Wesleyan began to lead me into an area of study that I hadn't anticipated. I was working for a degree in psychology in order to begin a career as a high school counselor. The psychology courses were supplemented with two required courses in religion.

I began to have casual discussions with Mom about what I was learning of religions of the world. Initially, I think I was simply eager to show off, to let someone in the family know that I was being exposed to new and different views about religion and theology.

The knowledge that I acquired at Wesleyan triggered a torrent of doubts and questions. I had been raised in a Christian home and my early lessons in church were being challenged. I didn't have the answers.

My discussions with Mom gradually grew into disagreements, then arguments. Some of my challenges to her beliefs were fostered by a change that I sensed in Dad. Before my accident, Dad always spoke confidently of God and his faith in God; now he said very little. He continued to do things for me and the rest of the family, but he seemed to have doubts. He had been tireless in seeking medical help and any aid that would make my life more complete. The effort had caught up with him. He looked tired. Problems at work added extra pressure. He kept everything bottled up until one of us would say something or do something that set him off. Then he'd sometimes react harshly and arguments and disagreements often resulted. He seemed to be lonely and unhappy. Yet I knew he was a Christian and his behavior puzzled me.

My arguments with Mom were more and more frequent. One afternoon, after a prolonged classroom discussion about Hinduism, I came home in an arrogant mood. I didn't have a faith and I felt that she had no valid reason for hers.

"Mom, how do you know that there's an eternal life with God? Who said so? And if you can't see God, how can you have faith in him?"

She was insulted and she reacted angrily for a moment. Then she got out her Bible and began to show me Scriptures that supported her beliefs.

Her finger ran down the page until it rested on a verse in the Book of John:

> For God so loved the world, that he gave his only begotten Son, that whosoever believeth in him should not perish, but have everlasting life (3:16).

She calmed down and rested her argument as she watched my eyes follow the words. I couldn't understand how words on a piece of paper could bring such comfort to a person.

I found it more and more difficult to argue successfully with her. Her very reaction to my challenges and her response with Scriptures frustrated me. Her confidence in her faith made me want to have those same feelings, but I didn't know how to reach for them and I wasn't positive that I wanted to trade the way I was living my life for them, if that's what it took.

I didn't know what I believed in or what I stood for.

Shortly before Daphne's graduation from nursing school in June 1972, I talked with Dad about my plan to marry Daphne. As we talked and I shared my excitement about my future, I sensed that he might be trying to shake off some of the melancholy he seemed to feel and find a reason to look forward to the future. I thought that perhaps the knowledge that I was confident enough to talk about my marriage plans helped.

He didn't question our love for each other or the wisdom of getting married or where we would live or how we would support each other. He was concerned, however, about my ability to continue to be covered by a hospitalization plan when I was no longer eligible under his policy. We both knew that I was likely to find myself in one again for any of a thousand reasons. When he learned that the coverage could be converted to my name, he gave us his blessing.

Daphne and I hadn't settled on a wedding date, but her graduation prompted an exchange of important gifts.

She was to start a full-time job as an emergency-room nurse at General Hospital of Virginia Beach and she needed a car. She discussed the possibilities with me and told me that she wanted to buy a van because it would be more convenient for my travels. After the van was purchased, Mr. Via made a wooden ramp for it, enabling me to be rolled in and out with ease.

A few days after Daphne bought the van, I called and asked her to come to the house earlier than usual. She was expected for dinner, but I had something that I wanted to give her.

Any time we had talked of an engagement, she said that she really didn't care about having a ring. But I knew that she was thinking of me and the fact that I had only the money that the family gave me.

I watched from the living room window until she drove up to the house. I wheeled to my room and was making a pretense of serious study when she came in.

"Hi, hon. What're you studying?" she asked, kissing me and taking a chair beside mine.

"Not much of anything right now. I can't."

"Why?" she asked.

"Because I'm thinking of you. And us. Daph, are you sure you wouldn't like an engagement ring?"

"No, Skip. I've told you that before. Why would you ask me that?"

"Because this is for you," I said, extending my hand toward her and opening it. "I hope you'll like it."

Her expression was all I could have asked for. She beamed.

"Oh, Skip. I love you so much! So very much. Where did you get it? How did you get it?"

I let the questions go unanswered as she hugged me.

14

Beginnings

Daphne and I sat close to each other as Tommy Viar's van rolled toward Elizabeth City, North Carolina. The date was September 23, 1972.

We were on our way to be married. We had decided to elope because Daphne didn't want to burden her parents with the expense of a wedding.

I reached frequently for Daphne's hand. Being able to touch her and sense her presence helped me contain the excitement that had been building since I awoke that morning. We had talked often during the past two and a half years about a life together. We had planned and we had dreamed. I was surprised now that our wedding day had arrived that there was still excitement to be savored. A mixture of pride, happiness, excitement, and a touch of apprehension bubbled up inside me.

The day was September-perfect. A steady breeze moved the trees and shrubbery in the churchyard. The sun shone down from a deep blue sky. Berea Baptist Church was a small, simple country church. It, too, seemed perfect for the ceremony.

Paul Bradley stood beside my chair as we waited for Daphne to come down the aisle with Tommy. "The Wedding March" was playing.

Daphne appeared at the far end of the aisle. She was more beautiful than I had ever seen her, more beautiful than any woman I had ever seen.

We clasped hands and looked at each other as the minister

started the ceremony. I tried to listen to all of the words, but I could only look at her and think how fortunate I was.

The minister had turned to her.

"Do you, Daphne Elizabeth Via, take this man, Alfred Thomas Wilkins, Jr., to be your lawful wedded husband . . . ?"

Husband. The word *husband.*

I heard the rest of the words he spoke and I remember thinking briefly that I was sitting in a wheelchair when he said, "in sickness and in health."

He had ended his question.

Daphne squeezed my hand hard and smiled down at me in a way that I would never forget.

"I do," she said. Her voice was so soft and yet so clear and proud.

I had never known such joy.

Our wedding day breakfast was really an early lunch at a hamburger stand on the way back to Virginia Beach.

When we arrived at home, we were taken, accompanied by fanfare from the family, to our new home. My room had been changed. Mom and Dad had given us their double bed, we had a small dining table and chairs, and furniture had been moved around to accommodate the small refrigerator that Daphne and I had bought.

We drove to the Vias and told them about our marriage. After their surprise subsided and the breathless questions of "when" and "where" and "how" were answered, they overwhelmed us with affection and wishes for happiness.

After dinner we all gathered in the living room. The conversation seemed endless and I kept looking at Daphne, wondering if it would be impolite to excuse ourselves.

Finally the conversations ended and we went to our apartment. I was as nervous as any bridegroom must be on his wedding night and I had an apprehension that many never know. I could respond only to direct physical stimulation and often, doctors had warned, even that would be difficult or unsuccessful.

Whether it was Daphne's medical background or our long discussions about my limitations or simply the fact that we loved each other so much, our first night together as man and wife had all the completeness, all the tenderness, and all of the emotion that any man and woman could have. She helped me erase any apprehensions I had about my paralysis and my physical ability to make love and to be loved.

Later I put my arms around her and she fell asleep. As I looked at her beside me in the dark quietness of our room, I had but one thought: how happy and how whole, emotionally and physically, the woman I was holding had made me feel. I hoped that I had given her, that night, the same happiness.

———————

As one year ended and another began, our life fell into a pattern dictated by Daphne's job and my classes. I was at Wesleyan usually until 1:30 in the afternoon. Daphne worked in the emergency room at Beach General on the three to eleven night shift. Our home life centered around lunchtime meals. Mom provided my dinners and helped me prepare for bed when Daphne worked. Our social life centered on high school sports activities. Karen was still a cheerleader and Shirley had become one, too. I took a lot of pride in them, especially Shirley, because I had encouraged her in her constant practices to make the squad. On some weekends, when Daphne was off, we'd go out to dinner with Karen and one of her boyfriends.

My proposed topic for my senior project had been approved. I was doing a comparative study of individuals' personal interests before and after suffering traumatic injuries. Most of my research was done at Woodrow Wilson and Daphne and I spent many weekends with Linda and Tommy at their apartment in nearby Charlottesville.

In March I learned that the Community Mental Health Center

in Norfolk was planning to open an adolescent day care center and was interviewing for a part-time case aide. The idea of a job that could fit into my schedule at school and that was in the field that I wanted to enter was exciting. But the problem of transportation appeared to be too big to solve.

I mentioned the possibility of the job to one of our friends, David Terry.

"That's great, Skip," he said. "If you get the job, I'd be willing to give you a ride to work." David worked at a large grocery store on the same street as the planned day care center.

I pursued the job and was selected. My first paycheck was for $45.23. The check wasn't a lot of money, but it was another boost to my confidence. It also provided an opportunity for Daphne and me to take Mom, Dad, Shirley, and Karen out to dinner.

As we chatted during dinner about the progress we had all made, I was sure that Dad was beginning to feel better about me, about my future, and about himself. He was beginning to share his thoughts and his feelings again with the rest of the family.

In late April our routine suddenly changed. I had decided to stay home from Wesleyan because I didn't feel well. Daphne had left in the morning for a nurses' meeting.

I had become sensitive to the slightest change in my body's behavior and I was getting signals that something was wrong. My heartbeat increased. I became slightly nauseous and felt slight chills.

I knew what to look for and I found it. Once again blood was in my urine. David arrived, saw that I was sick, and offered his help. Within hours, David, Mom, and I were headed to Norfolk General Hospital in his car.

The next morning the X rays pinpointed the reason for the latest sickness: both ureters, the tubes that carry urine from the kidneys to the bladder, were badly swollen.

When Dr. Poutasse came into my room, I knew immediately that he was concerned. We had been through so many crises together that we had come to know each other well.

"Skip," he said, "we've got some trouble this time. A TUR isn't going to get us through this one. Your bladder is stretched so badly that it can't function. The urine is backing up well into the kidneys and they aren't able to drain. We have to get them to drain."

No TUR, I thought. *Then, what?* My mind reeled at the thought of what might have to be done.

"How?" I asked. "What . . . has to be done?" I really didn't want to hear the answer.

"I want to try a suprapubic. That requires a catheter inserted directly into the bladder right above the pubic area. We won't go through the penis again."

"No. No. There's got to be something else. I'm married. I can't do it."

"Skip. Skip, just take it easy." He knew that I was agitated and his voice became soothing.

"We've got to do it. And I can't guarantee that this will work. But if it does, you don't have to worry about sex. Or anything else. It'll be less of a problem all the way around. Think about it. And take it easy. I'll see you tomorrow."

As the door shut, I closed my eyes. I didn't want another operation of any kind. I didn't want to be in the hospital. I wanted to leave. To go home and be with Daphne.

He hadn't told me what would happen if this new operation wasn't successful. But I knew. I had heard it called an ileostomy at Fishersville. The thought of it made me cringe. A bag attached to my side, constantly filling and needing to be emptied by someone because I couldn't use my hands very well. That and pressure sores were the biggest horrors for a quadriplegic. Each destroyed whatever dignity was left. Especially the bag. The need to have someone always empty it. And it could leak. Or break.

Mom came in.

"It's going to be all right," she said.

"No, Mom, I can't have it done. Not since being married. It's only been six months. I can't."

"Skip," her voice was firm, "if this has to be done, you'll have to have it done. Daphne knows. Dr. Poutasse has talked to her. She understands and she agrees with him."

"No." I was angry. "Please just leave me alone."

As she retreated to the door, I glanced down at the bed-bag, now half filled with red-tinted urine, reminding me of the problem.

I was thinking about the operation, trying to visualize the tube protruding from a hole in my stomach, when Daphne came in.

She didn't say anything; she just looked at me. Always, when she looked at me, I wanted to be strong and make her proud. This time it was hard to do.

"Daph, did he tell you what they want to do to me?"

"Yes, he told me. But don't worry. It's going to work. It will be better for us to live with. I know something about it."

"Are you just saying that? Do you really believe that? I don't know, Daph."

"I believe it, Skip. Just think. No more problems. No more worrying about when you'll get sick again. No more difficulty with your kidneys draining. It's going to be so much better."

Her acceptance of what was going to be done helped. If she believed things would be better, then I had to believe, too.

I had the operation on May 1. That night the blood started to clear from my urine. Two days later I went home. Dr. Poutasse told me that he would run tests on me in August to check the condition of my bladder. I was able to push the thought of a bag, always taped over the drainage opening in my side, out of my mind.

Wayne Whitley had joined Daphne and me for my last trip to Fishersville. I was headed to Woodrow Wilson for a final confer-

ence on the data I had collected for my senior project and I was
going to take part in a bowling and pool-shooting exhibition by
the disabled, all at Woodrow Wilson. The exhibition was new to
me and I had decided to enter since I had to be at the center
anyway. In addition, I had gotten pretty good at bowling with
Daphne since my final hand operation and I still spent time
shooting pool with the friends who came to visit us.

When I reported to the center early that Saturday morning for
the competition, I was told to check in with the doctor.

"Why?" I asked.

"You need to be classified," I was told.

The doctor put me through the same series of tests I had undergone so frequently during hospital stays. He tested my re-
flexes, my muscle control, and the degree of paralysis throughout
my body. I paid little attention when the doctor finally told me
that I would participate as a "1A." I would learn later that 1A was
the classification for the most severely damaged athletes.

The bowling was as relaxing as bowling with Daphne at our
local bowling alley. It didn't seem like an athletic event. And the
pool-shooting was as enjoyable as shooting pool in the garage.

At the end of the weekend's events, I was awarded a first place
in bowling and a second place in pool. Daphne was more excited
about the medals than I was. I was impressed, however, with
what I had heard about the track and field competition that had
been held for the disabled. When we returned home, she hung
the two medals in our apartment.

On my return from Fishersville, I made the last corrections
and changes in my thesis and submitted it to my psychology professor. I began sorting my notes and studying for final exams. My
grades were above the requirements needed to graduate and I
wanted to end my college career on the highest note I could
reach.

Several days later I sat outside the administration building
waiting for graduation practice to begin. I would be the first person in the Wilkins family to graduate from college. I thought back
over the problems and successes of the past five years. Two work-

men began building a ramp to the platform as I watched. I knew that the ramp was for me. I thought of the pride that my diploma would bring to the family. Dad had worked tirelessly to insure an education for me. Linda and Mom had driven me to and from class so many times. Shirley and Karen had copied and typed countless assignments for me. Daphne and her belief in our future had become the greatest reasons for a sense of pride.

The professor coordinating the rehearsal called for attention. He explained that those seniors receiving diplomas would walk onto the stage, accept their diplomas from President Clarke and return to their seats.

He explained that the seniors who would not receive diplomas because of incomplete grades would be recognized and would cross the stage and shake hands with President Clarke.

He began to call out the list of those who would receive diplomas. As he worked his way through the alphabet toward the W's, I could feel the anticipation building.

"Roy Preston White."

My name was next.

"Rex Victor Willard."

He had skipped my name.

I suddenly wondered if I'd been skipped because I hadn't completed the oral defense of my research paper before the faculty committee. I had been late with my paper because I'd been in the hospital. I couldn't remember if my psychology professor had said anything about the orals. I didn't think he had.

The professor in charge of rehearsal began to call out the list of seniors who would be recognized, but who would not receive diplomas.

My name was on that list.

I located one of my professors.

It was the orals. I would have an incomplete grade until I presented my defense of my research. I could make the arrangements immediately after graduation and my diploma would be mailed to me.

I was dumbfounded. Not graduate? No diploma? How could I face anyone in the family? I rolled away from the practice and fought back tears. The thought of having to tell Mom was the pain that I felt now.

She was coming from the car to help me down the hill. She knew something was wrong.

"Skip, are you sick?"

"No, Mom. I'm not sick. It's worse. I'm not going to graduate with the rest of my class."

Mom was in shock at the words I had just spoken.

But the shock quickly left.

"What!" She didn't say it like a question. It was an exclamation. "What!" Then came the question. "Why?" I could see she was getting angry.

"Mom, I can't get my diploma because I haven't done my orals on my paper. I didn't know that. I can go through the ceremony, but I won't get my diploma until later."

"There's a mistake. There must be. I'm sure of it. I'm going to straighten this out right now. I'm going to see somebody. Where's the office?"

I tried to stop her.

"No, Mom. Please don't. Forget it. Let's just go."

But she was already headed toward the administration building.

The meeting had been civil, but just barely.

She didn't talk to me on the drive home. She told me later that she was trying to remember what had been said so she could give an accurate report to Dad.

She said she hadn't lost her temper when she entered the office; she'd only managed to control it.

When she had repeated what I had told her to the man behind the desk he had carefully explained the requirements for the senior project and the obligation of each student to schedule and complete an oral defense of the paper.

"I understand that, sir. But my son was sick for more than a week. Can't he take the examinations now? Before graduation? We've worked so hard for this. All of us. Isn't there some way he can?

"Mrs. Wilkins, I'm terribly sorry. I am. But we have to operate with certain requirements. They apply to everyone."

"I can't believe that. He's met every requirement. Except this oral thing. He's worked hard. He deserves to graduate with his class. It means so much to him. To all of us."

"Mrs. Wilkins, I'm sorry. We cannot change the rules. Your son has never asked special consideration since he's been here. We have to operate Virginia Wesleyan College with rules that apply equally to everyone. I cannot make an exception in your son's case. Please try to keep in mind that he will receive his diploma as soon as he has completed his oral defense of his paper."

"No!"

Mom wasn't exactly sure what the man had said then. She was getting more upset. She thought she had heard something about "adjust to things," but she couldn't be sure.

Adjust? What does he think we've been doing? she asked herself.

She prayed hard not to give in to her impulse to lash out and looked one final time at the man behind the desk.

Then she turned and strode out, not bothering to shut the door as she left.

The family was crushed at the news about graduation. I was embarrassed about not completing my oral defense on time and I was hurt because the family had been hurt. I couldn't bring myself to attend the graduation ceremonies. I went through my oral defense three days after the ceremony and passed without difficulty.

We weren't able to put the incident out of our minds until my diploma arrived in the mail. Mom was still hurt, but the receipt of the diploma began to mellow the rest of the family's feelings. I had, after all, graduated from college. And that was good reason to celebrate.

I began to look back on my two years at Wesleyan with real appreciation. The professors had worked with me and helped me deal with some of my inabilities. A number of the students had become friends. I had a solid college education. I had become genuinely interested in understanding more about religion. And I had made it on my own. I had a right to be proud of myself. On top of all that, I now had a full-time job as a counselor at the day care center.

August came and with it my appointment with Dr. Poutasse for an examination to determine whether or not my bladder had returned to its normal size.

I had been feeling great all summer and there had been no problem with the suprapubic. But the thought of another IVP and what the results could mean brought back the worry of what could happen. I began to handle the fear differently. I prayed. I wasn't confident that God was going to hear or answer my prayers because I wasn't sure of my relationship with him. But I felt I needed a miracle to heal my bladder. I acknowledged that my relationship with God was weak, but I believed that he alone could help me.

The IVP had been completed and I was lying on the X-ray table waiting for Dr. Poutasse to tell me the results. I was trying to decide how to express my gratitude if the X rays revealed that I wouldn't have to have the operation that I feared the most: the ileal conduit. From somewhere, I had developed enough faith that God would help me through this to wonder about how to respond to him.

"God," I prayed. "If everything turns out all right, I'll praise you right here."

Dr. Poutasse came in, carrying two X rays.

"Skip," he said, "I can't believe this. Your kidneys have returned to normal size again. It is incredible."

Before he could show me the pictures or say another word, I said in a loud, strong voice, "Praise the Lord."

"You can say that again. There is no way that this should have happened. Do you know how close you were to serious kidney disease?"

It didn't matter how close I had been. The operation had been avoided. I had prayed to God as well as I knew how and my prayers were answered.

While the miracle of my healed bladder and kidneys gave Daphne and me cause for rejoicing, many of the little details of our life began to irritate me. Daphne had taken a new job and was driving me to work. My dependence on her began to bother me. I was often impatient with her when she helped me to dress in the morning. My temper flared more often than it ever had.

An argument about dinner one night climaxed when I slammed my fist to the table, causing a dish to fall to the floor and shatter.

Daphne broke into tears. She sat helpless and crying at the table. I wheeled out of the house to calm down. I couldn't understand why I had behaved in such a way. It wasn't my nature, yet it was as though there were some force inside me that compelled me to become angry and to hurt her.

Still without an answer as to why I had become so enraged, I returned to her and apologized as sincerely as I could. I told her that it wouldn't happen again. But I wasn't sure I could live up to that promise. I didn't know what was happening to me, but I wanted to find the answer.

I was on a roller coaster for the next few months. My temper would subside, then erupt. I had doubts about my future and what I should do with my life. I clung to the miracle that had happened in the X-ray room. It gave me at times the strength and the courage to suppress the doubts about my life and the guilt of my arguments with Daphne and others.

I began to realize that some of my troubled feelings came from the frustration of being able to do little for myself. Daphne took care of me almost totally. I had been building up resentment because I couldn't help myself, much less do things for my wife.

Slowly I began to bring my temper under better control and I ceased to become frustrated over little things that I couldn't do for myself. But I was lacking peace. I didn't feel that my life was being lived as fully as it could be.

Over and over I analyzed my circumstances. Physically, I was healthy. More importantly, I had no apprehensions about my medical future, now that the bladder problem apparently had been solved. My goals, the ones I had stated so long ago in a newspaper interview, had been achieved. I had worked hard and earned a college education. I was married. I had a full-time job. But something was missing.

Each time that I thought about my life and searched for an answer, I found myself thinking of Christianity and what I had learned about it from my studies and reading, from my parents and from Sunday school and church: a belief in God and in his Son, who died for me and for my sins and promised eternal life. As a child I had been brought up to believe, but as a teenager and as an adult, I called on God only when I desperately needed him. I always felt that I would be required to give up something in return for his help. I didn't like the idea.

My attitude gradually shifted from doubt to a hope that perhaps Christianity was the answer that would bring me peace and a full life. The thought became constant during the fall and into the last months of 1973.

I had no major crisis. There was no single dramatic incident that led me. It happened one night at home with Daphne. I told her that I was going to set aside all my doubts and fears and that I was going to ask for forgiveness and the help of Christ. I realized that never before had I asked forgiveness or sought a purpose to my life. Help, yes. But not forgiveness. Not purpose.

I prayed that night in our bedroom. No bells rang. No light flashed. No cannon sounded. Something more telling happened. I sensed deep within myself that for the first time in my life I was being honest with God and with myself. I needed help; but more than that, I needed forgiveness.

That night I felt that a great weight, a weight that had pressed down on me for so long, had been lifted from my shoulders. I experienced an inner peace that I had never known.

As I closed my eyes for sleep to come, I acknowledged that God and his mercy had not changed, but that I had changed.

15

New Directions

A trip to Fishersville, Virginia, in May 1974, marked more changes in my life.

Before Linda, Tommy, and Daphne got into the car, they helped me into the driver's seat. I was a licensed driver. Dad and a family friend had installed hand controls in a 1969 Buick Electra, a gift from my uncle, Cle Wilkins.

We were headed to Fishersville where I would participate in competitive track and field events in the Virginia Wheelchair Games. I had received a registration form in the mail because of my participation the year before in exhibition bowling and pool. After looking over the forms, I had decided to enter the shot put, 40-yard dash, table tennis, and the slalom race—an obstacle course for wheelchair athletes. All for the first time. I'd played a little table tennis with the youngsters at the day care center and with friends since the accident and I had heard about the track and field competition when I had last visited Woodrow Wilson. But that was all I knew of what was in store for me.

When the competition began early Saturday morning, I experienced feelings that I thought would never be possible again for me. The same sense of exhilaration that I had known in my high school athletics came back to me. There was constant activity on the field and I was fascinated by the varied techniques and forms of the others in wheelchairs as they limbered up.

As I rolled into the throwing circle, my heart beat faster and I

had the same churning stomach that always had been there before the gun sounded in a race or before the opening kickoff in a
football game. The shot was awkward and I had a difficult time
trying to balance it for the first throw. When it landed, the small
crowd that had gathered to watch the competition responded
with applause and shouts.

I didn't know how far I had thrown, but the fact that I had been
able to throw and that the crowd had reacted were rewards
enough. I made my last two throws and left the circle. The official
told me that I was in first place going into the finals later in the
day.

In the finals, I improved with each of my three throws. I was
overwhelmed when the official told me that I had unofficially
broken a national record, as well as winning the event. As I signed
the record sheet, the official asked me if I planned to compete in
the national games in June. I had never heard of them, but I was
encouraged by Linda, Tommy, and Daphne, who were as excited
as I was.

"Yes, I guess so. I'd like to. What do I have to do?" I asked.

He explained that registration forms would be available the
next day for the games in Washington.

In the hotel room, I rested between events, waiting for the table tennis competition. The scenes of the morning played over
and over in my mind: the determined faces of the competitors;
athletes in colorful warmups or, like me, in casual street clothes
and tennis shoes; the officials who had been so helpful and encouraging to each competitor; the thrill of competing again and
winning. I thanked God for allowing me to become excited again
about athletics.

That night I added another victory to my first venture into
competitive wheelchair sports when I won the table tennis event.
Daphne and I rushed to a telephone to tell Mom and Dad about
my performances. They were as happy as we were and they assured me that the whole family would drive up to Washington to
see me compete in the national games.

As the excitement of the day ebbed, Linda, Daphne, and I talked quietly in the hotel room.

"Linda," I said, "for the first time in my life I have a peace with God."

"You know, Skip, I prayed and accepted God right after your accident, but sometimes I still have doubts."

"I know. So do I. But I think that's normal. What is most important is that we know in our hearts what we believe."

Daphne had been quiet, listening to us. Linda turned to her.

"What about you, Daph, are you a Christian?"

She was startled. "I guess so. I've gone to church."

"But have you ever asked God into your heart? Have you been saved?" Linda asked.

"I don't know about things like that. I don't think I'm a bad person the way I am now."

The three of us began to talk about salvation as we understood it, seeking answers to our questions in a Gideon Bible that had been on the night table. The Bible listed a series of questions about the Christian life and cited Scriptures in providing the answers.

We talked a long time. Finally Daphne turned to me.

"Well, I need salvation because I want to be in heaven with you, Skip. What should I do?"

We turned again to the Bible and read aloud the steps that were outlined. The three of us then closed our eyes and Daphne said a prayer, asking for forgiveness and salvation. I was moved very much by what had happened and I was happy for Daphne because of my own experience.

Linda left to rejoin Tommy in their room.

Daphne talked for a while.

"I don't feel any different, Skip. Am I supposed to? I do know that what I just did feels right."

"Let's just take it slowly," I responded, "like I've been doing. Like we've been doing. A step at a time."

That night, we prayed together. It was a short prayer and perhaps awkwardly worded, but it was a prayer offered for the first time by the two of us as husband and wife.

On our drive home I received a disappointing lesson in geography. Daphne was reading the registration forms for the national games as we headed back to Virginia Beach. The nationals would be held in Cheney, Washington, not Washington, D.C., as I had assumed and as I had told Dad on the phone.

It was a blow. "That's all-the-way-on-the-West-Coast Washington," I sighed. "We can't go there. It would cost a fortune."

Beth Polson and her newspaper, however, helped us overcome the problems of distance and dollars. She wrote a story about my performance at Fishersville and my interest in going to the nationals. Individuals and businessmen responded to the story with financial contributions. I opened a travel account and Ran Randolph, a vice president at the bank, became interested in me and began to help me with the accounting.

Before I left for the West Coast, Karen received her diploma from Princess Anne. As we celebrated, I was reminded again of how close we were as a family.

Daphne and I boarded the plane for Spokane, Washington, on June 14. Neither of us had traveled such a distance from home and we wondered what we would find when we landed on the West Coast. We had packed every item that I would possibly need. In some cases, we carried two similar items each in a different bag in case one bag was lost. The last item that I put in the suitcase was my Bible. Daily, I spent a quiet time reading and studying.

The pleasure of traveling together to a new place was rapidly giving way to fatigue and the shock of changing time zones when Daphne pulled the rental car into a parking space at Eastern Washington University, the site of the games. Daphne rolled my chair to me and I noticed that my cushion wasn't in the chair. I had reminded her about the cushion when I had transferred from the chair into the car at the airport. I had last seen it resting on the rear of the car before we pulled away.

"Daphne, where is the cushion?" I asked.

She was quick to respond.

"Haven't you got it? I thought you picked it up before we left the airport."

I lost my temper. "You better have it. Or you better find it. I told you to take care of it." I was scared. The idea of sitting for any length of time, much less competing, without the cushion was alarming. It was as much a requirement to meet my basic needs as water and food. It was part of an arsenal of special equipment; it helped prevent pressure sores. I became angry enough to want to strike out at something. So I did. I rammed my elbow into the car door. Hard. Then again. I completely lost control of myself. Daphne was close to tears. I was embarrassed at my childish reaction to the missing cushion and my elbow ached, but neither feeling erased the fear of sitting for days without a cushion.

We drove back to the airport, searched the area where we had picked up the car, and inquired inside the terminal. No cushion.

We were exhausted. It was 2 A.M. on the West Coast and 5 A.M. back home. We didn't know where our room was and we couldn't find anyone awake at the college. Daphne's tears finally came. Someone eventually helped us find a vacant room. We had been up for nearly twenty-four hours. But the beds, typical of some college dorms, were only a foot or so high. I didn't think that I could successfully transfer into one of them. And if I could, I wondered how I would get out. We called Dad, who said that he would put another cushion on a plane that morning.

We finally managed to lie down. We were tired and frustrated. This wasn't what I had envisioned when the official back in Virginia had asked me if I planned to compete in the national games. I didn't even pray. I was simply and totally defeated.

In the morning, after a little sleep, we promised each other that we would make the best of our situation. We both prayed. I asked forgiveness for my actions and we prayed for the safe arrival of the second cushion and the strength to pull ourselves together.

When we registered, we were moved into a room with higher beds. We began to meet a number of athletes and we studied the schedule of events.

I had developed a small open wound on my rear from sitting so long without the cushion the night before. Daphne suggested that I continue to lie down that afternoon and rest while she drove to the airport to get the second cushion.

She remained away for a long time and when she finally returned, I could tell from her expression that there was no cushion. I lashed at her again. She had looked everywhere at the airport for the cushion. She even started back to the baggage claim area, but the airline agent had told her that he had checked and it wasn't there.

I rode with her as she drove for the third time to the terminal.

In the baggage claim area, slowly making its circular journey on the conveyor belt, was the cushion.

Again that night we tried to calm ourselves, but my prayers became questions. Why were we being confronted with only problems? Why would God make this experience so difficult after all that I had been through?

There was another worry the next day as competition began. The heat was intense, sapping my strength and making me dizzy. I lost in the third round of table tennis and had to struggle to win the consolation match and a bronze medal.

I faced the same kind of heat the following day. Daphne was my only ally. She was my trainer, my coach, and my cheerleader. She tried to cool me down with ice packs on my head and my neck between events. At the end of the day's trials in the field events, I knew that it wasn't going to be like my entry into wheelchair sports back in Fishersville. I was out of the running in the slalom. I did, however, hold first place in the shot put trials.

Daphne and I relaxed for the first time the night before the finals. We had been through a tough time on our first trip together. The experience had been so unpleasant that I questioned whether winning a first place—still a possibility in the shot— would make up for all the heartache.

I was denied the victory. I remained in first place until the next-to-last competitor's name was called—Rod Vleiger, who had beaten me in table tennis. On his last attempt, he bettered my mark. I was next up and, despite the best effort I could give, I didn't overtake him. I was awarded the silver.

Daphne knew that I was depressed as we headed for the room after the meet. She tried to bolster my spirits.

"You shouldn't feel so badly, Skip. It's only your first year. I think you really did well."

"I know it's my first year. But I wanted to win. This trip has been terrible. You haven't had any fun. Neither have I. I've had all the traveling that I ever want to do. I just want to go home."

I was defeated physically, emotionally, and spiritually. The two medals that I had won weren't enough to remove the bitter taste of defeat and dejection as we headed back to the East Coast and home.

Our misadventures and my defeats in Washington received a variety of antidotes when we got home.

Physically, my biggest concern was the small wound that had opened on my posterior. I knew about pressure sores and what such sores could do, even in a nonathletic life, so I was apprehensive when the doctor examined me. He told me that the wound wasn't on a pressure area and prescribed a medicated cream and confinement to bed for five days. The wound finally closed, leaving a calloused spot on my rear and a frequent worry in my mind because the callus didn't disappear.

Emotionally, Daphne and I had been out of control. But from the experience, we had learned a lot about ourselves under stress and we knew that we had to be on constant guard against striking out at each other for any reason. We had grown closer as a result of facing difficulties together, but we were aware that we had a lot to learn about communicating with each other and about living a Christian life together.

The deepest wound from the Washington trip was spiritual. I hadn't behaved in a Christian way. I had responded to minor problems with outrage. My faith had vanished when the circumstances became adverse. It began to dawn on me that I equated belief with the ability to say a prayer and to look for an answer. I began to look at the way I lived my whole life. As I did, I realized that I couldn't pray for situations always to be pleasant, but I could seek God's help in handling such situations in a different way. I recognized that I was weak and that I needed God's strength to help me change. I began to read the Bible more thoughtfully, seeking Scriptures that would help me change. I shared these feelings and these efforts with Daphne. Together, we began to feel good about ourselves and about my effort to learn more about God's desires for our lives.

A celebration was called for in the summer. Dad and a friend had completed work on a new bass boat for me. They had mounted the seat and backrest assembly of a wheelchair on a swiveled pedestal in the boat. The seat gave me the mobility to drive the boat from a secure position, reducing the possibility that I might fall over the side. The boat was fourteen feet long with sixty-eight-inch beam and a fifty horsepower motor mounted on the transom. Using the specially designed crane and pulley to board and leave the boat, I was now able to travel anywhere on the Sound in search of bass. The boat was fast enough to use for pulling skiers and I once again was part of the family's enjoyment of the water. Another dream realized!

Now that I could drive a car and get around on my own, Daphne and I turned our thoughts to her professional needs. Her job with the Health Department in Norfolk was convenient, but it didn't offer the clinical work that she enjoyed so much. We decided to work toward a more personally rewarding job for her.

In addition to clinical and administrative opportunities, the job also had to offer day hours and weekends off so that we could be together as much as possible. We were determined that our family life always would be our first consideration.

Daphne took the required exams for nurses' openings in civil service and was placed on a hiring list.

Within two weeks, she received the offer of a position with an impressive increase in salary. The hours, however, called for night work and alternate weekend duty. We agonized over the decision and prayed for guidance. Finally, in spite of the tempting salary, she declined.

We wondered for days whether it had been the right decision. We continued to pray. The next telephone call she received was the offer of a position at the Norfolk Naval Air Station Dispensary. The days and hours were perfect, the salary was higher than the job she had declined, and she was able to ride to and from work with Dad, whose office was nearby on the Naval Base. In October Daphne returned to the kind of nursing practice she most enjoyed.

I began to feel more confident, now that both of us were growing as Christians. We had faced a lot of problems, big and small. Some we handled well, with God's help. Other times we fell flat on our faces and had to pick ourselves up and begin again. But I knew that our lives had changed for the better, and I received an important piece of evidence soon after Daphne began her new job.

Angie Spruill worked with me at Community Mental Health. We talked frequently about the challenges of our jobs and the different counseling approaches needed for the individual children in our care. There was always pressure.

One day Angie asked me, "Skip, how come you are handling the problems here so calmly? You seem to be different from the way you were when you first came to work."

"It's all in God's hands, Angie. He's the One who guides me now."

She wanted me to explain. As I began to talk about finding my faith, she shared her fears and her confusion.

"I've looked so long for the kind of peace that you have," she said.

With that brief conversation as a beginning, Angie and I began a Bible study together. Another co-worker joined us. I felt that we were giving and receiving strength from each other and, in some way, doing God's work with him.

The opportunity to touch more people came in February 1975, after a pleasant evening in my parents' home. Our pastor, Dick Woodward, and his wife were dinner guests. The family had started attending his church, Virginia Beach Community Chapel, in 1973. Dick Woodward had visited me in Norfolk General shortly after the accident, and I remembered his kindness and concern.

During the after-dinner conversations, Dick became very interested in my feelings about the accident and how I had begun to find my faith. We talked for a long time.

Before he left, he asked, "Skip, would you mind sharing your life with others?"

I wasn't sure what he had in mind, but I said that I would be happy to do it. He said that he would like for me to speak to the congregation at a Sunday morning service.

I was flattered that he felt I had something to contribute, but I was also nervous. Nearly seven hundred people attended the Sunday service at Community Chapel.

My anxiety about speaking soon mixed with the anticipation of sharing my life with so many others.

When I looked out over the congregation on that Sunday, I saw the faces of many people who had helped me and my family. It was comforting. I began to tell them the story.

I wasn't able to reflect much on my speaking when I went to the social hall after the service. Hundreds of people came to me and told me how much they appreciated what I had said and that they had gained a stronger personal faith because of my story.

At home, I thought back on my talk. I was pleased that other people liked what I had said. More importantly, I was thankful that God wanted others to hear about my thoughts and my faith.

Several days later, Dick Woodward asked me to consider becoming the youth pastor at Community Chapel, to help meet the spiritual needs of the young people in the congregation.

I was hesitant. "I don't know that much about the Bible and formal study. I'm still learning."

"I understand that, Skip," Dick responded. "We can teach you those things. If God wants you in this ministry, you will know."

I weighed the offer at Community Chapel. Tentatively at first and then with certainty, I came to the realization that I needed and wanted much more understanding of God's Word. My initial response to Dick Woodward—"I don't know that much about the Bible"—became a goal of learning. There was no further discussion about the youth ministry and that possibility passed. But it left me with the feeling that God had given me a direction.

16

First Steps

One path to a greater understanding of the Bible led me to a kind and mild-mannered man named Ozzie Pretzman. He was an active member of Community Chapel and had heard me ask for prayer about going into God's work at a Sunday school dinner. He asked to visit. The next morning, before I had gotten up, Ozzie was sitting at the foot of my bed, asking me about my life as a Christian and about my study of the Bible. His interest in me and his vast knowledge of the Bible made me realize that I had a growing faith in God, but that I didn't have a clear understanding of that faith or how to strengthen it.

He came to the point of his visit.

"Would you like to know more, Skip, that will help you understand and build your faith in God?"

I was eager to study with him. Before he left, he gave me two assignments. The first, he said, was the most important. It was to learn John 14:26. This, he said, was the key to begin Bible study. The second assignment was a two-lesson Bible study.

"Call me, Skip, if, and when, you are ready to take the first step," he said.

By the day's end, I had read, reread, and memorized the verse from John:

But the Counselor, the Holy Spirit, whom the Father will send in my name, will teach you all things and will remind you of everything I have said to you.

I also completed both of the study lessons. I not only was ready for the next meeting with Ozzie, I was eager.

By mid-April I was deeply involved with Ozzie in a study of the Word. Daphne had joined me and together we marveled at the discoveries we made as we learned the Bible's messages.

One evening, Wayne Whitley called to ask me to serve as a reference for him. He had learned that the City of Virginia Beach soon would open a short-term adolescent crisis care facility; he wanted to apply for one of the counselor positions. He told me that the city was looking for a director and an assistant director. Wayne knew that there were increasing problems at Community Mental Health where I worked. Some involved funding and others involved the counseling programs. So he encouraged me to apply for one of the new positions. I barely met the application deadline for assistant director or chief counselor, and was told that a decision would be made within the next two weeks.

A few weeks later, we headed toward Fishersville and the 1975 regional wheelchair meet. I thought back to the difficulties that Daphne and I had experienced in Washington the year before. I hadn't been certain that I would ever travel or compete again after the trip to Cheney. But many people had encouraged me to keep trying. Bill Taylor, a local businessman and a friend from Community Chapel, and his brother offered to sponsor travel for Daphne and me to regional meets and nationals, if I qualified. Martha Willey, who with her family owned a sporting goods store, had provided me with practice equipment: shot, javelin and discus (two new events for me), and warmup suits and shoes. Their support added to my incentive to do well. I worked out in our front yard with Shirley providing encouragement and retrieving my throws. Although my practices weren't very formal, I won the shot, the discus, the javelin, and table tennis at Fishersville and easily qualified for the nationals.

Mom and Dad saw me compete for the first time at Fishersville. Dad didn't say a lot at the end of the meet, but he had a smile that I hadn't seen in a long time. He had witnessed something that he hadn't thought would ever happen: my return to athletics. He was proud of the medals, but the fact that I was competing again was his greatest reward. His doubts about my future were fading.

As I started pulling myself back up in the athletic world, however, my work world came crashing down on me and all of my colleagues. Each of us was called into the administrator's office in mid-May and told that the Community Mental Health program would be terminated at month's end. I was almost relieved at the news; conflicts and program problems had gotten out of hand. Even though I had now lost my job and had long since given up hearing from the adolescent crisis care home, I believed Daphne and I would survive the setback. Calling Daphne, I told her the news and headed for Granny and Papa's place at Carolina where I could think about the future.

That evening Daphne called. She was so excited that she hardly could get the words out. The administrator of the Crisis Home for adolescents in Virginia Beach had called to explain that the staffing effort had fallen behind, but they now were ready to begin selecting employees. He wanted to know whether I was still interested in being interviewed. She relayed to him my very positive response and had set up an appointment.

Wayne appeared at Carolina the next morning. He had heard about my loss of a job, and Daphne had suggested to him that I might enjoy his companionship. Wayne and I had drifted apart after my marriage. The few days together, just the two of us fishing and remembering old times and talking about our lives, brought us close together again.

Wayne drove with me to my interview. Before the questions started, Bob Dunsmore, regional administrator for the program that would include the Crisis Home, explained to me that the operation of the home initially would not require an assistant director or a head counselor. He wanted to interview me for the director's position, based on my previous work, if I was interested in that. I quietly said a prayer that the wisdom and the experience I had gained would be sufficient for the job.

Near the end of the interview, he paused for a few moments.

"Skip," he said, "I'm very much impressed with your insight

into young people and your knowledge of counseling. You've also got the kind of experience that I'm looking for to develop this program. I've got to ask you a tough question, but an obvious one, about your physical limitations."

He explained that the home would be quartered in a two-story building. Sleeping accommodations for some of the youngsters would be on the second floor.

"How will you get to the second floor when you are needed there?"

I didn't have an immediate solution, but I did have a response.

"If you feel that I can handle the unknown problems that will come up with the kids, I feel that I can find an answer to this problem that we both know exists."

It wasn't a direct answer to the question, but I truly believed that if this job were meant for me, I could find a solution. I was not going to be defeated because of a wheelchair.

Interviews with other candidates were to continue through the week. Four people would be selected for final interviews before a committee.

Wayne and I returned to Carolina. Two days later Daphne called.

"Skip, the Crisis Home called you for the group interview. You're going to get that job. I just know you are."

That night I thanked God for giving me the ability and the knowledge to progress with the interviews as far as I had.

The committee interview was exacting. Their questions covered everything from religion to drugs, from sex among teenagers to a family's role in rearing children. I came away with a feeling that I had been responsive to the questions and had impressed the four members of the committee.

My feeling was confirmed the next evening as Wayne and I prepared to head out in the boat.

Granny hollered to me that Daphne was on the phone.

Daphne was almost breathless.

"Skip, you got the job. Mr. Dunsmore just called. He asked me to call you. You were the unanimous choice of the committee.

You're the *director* of the Crisis Intervention Home."

I listened in near disbelief. I had known that I was reaching high in trying for the directorship of a brand-new agency. And suddenly, I had grasped what I was reaching for. It took a moment for me to absorb what I had heard.

Daphne said that she would join me for the weekend as soon as she could, but that she wanted me to know right away how proud and how happy she was.

The national games in Champaign, Illinois, were scheduled to end only four days before I was to begin my job as director. This meet was vastly different from the nationals in Washington the year before. There was no lost cushion, no loss of temper and no angry words. My attitude was one of thankfulness that I was able to compete. Physically, I was better prepared for the events. At the end of the trials I was in first place in the shot, second in the javelin, and third in the discus. I made it into the finals of table tennis, but was defeated by Rod Vleiger, the same athlete who had beaten me the year before. I wanted a gold medal. I especially wanted to beat Rod in the shot. But I was motivated more by a desire to have a good attitude than by a desire for personal glory, thanks to my studies with Ozzie.

Before the close of the final events, I won two silver medals, in discus and javelin. And in the shot, I beat Rod and broke the national record that he had set the year before. I won the gold.

In addition, I was nominated for the U.S. team which would compete in Mexico. I wasn't selected, but I had done the best I could. That was satisfaction enough.

After the Washington meet, Daphne and I had almost given up; I had nearly quit athletics. Now I knew that I'd be back to compete in 1976 and that I had the same chance as anyone else to make the U.S. team and to compete in world competition.

When I got home, I became totally absorbed in my new job. Many of the responsibilities of directing the Crisis Home, as it came into being, were new to me.

The home was designed to be a short-term residential facility for children who had not committed criminal offenses, but who caused problems at home or in school. Repeated runaways, truants, and similarly troubled youngsters were to be in our care. The courts referred to them as "status offenders" and the home was to provide an alternative to the area detention homes, where they had to mingle with true lawbreakers.

Our mission was to provide a "cooling off" period away from the cause of the problem. We were to try to open up communication with the children, provide counseling when it was warranted, and return them to their homes and classrooms after their particular crisis had passed.

I relied on guidance from Bob and his assistant as I interviewed and hired a full staff and began to operate the home. I hired Wayne as one of the counselors, based on his past experiences at the juvenile detention home. The varied backgrounds and experiences of the staff gave me confidence that we could successfully help the young people who were sent to the home. From the outset, I tried to foster a work environment that allowed us to share our strengths and overcome our weaknesses as a cohesive group. It was not always easy or pleasant, but even in the early days of our work, we had a sense of openness and fellowship. The Virginia Department of Rehabilitation was a big help. Based on my employment and my limitations, the department provided a ramp to my office and a stair elevator to the second floor.

I had to appear frequently in court on behalf of some of our young wards, and visit other facilities affiliated with the city's juvenile program. The Department of Rehabilitation also was instrumental in helping me meet the need that presented. Through its efforts I purchased a van, and a local firm outfitted it with an electronically operated side door and wheelchair lift. I was able to get in and out of the van and to transfer from the wheelchair to the driver's seat without help. The final barrier to an independent life had fallen.

As the fall of 1975 arrived, I was responding almost solely to the demands of the Crisis Home. I spent long hours in the office dealing with daily problems and almost always took administrative paperwork home. Soon we were functioning at capacity, and the home had a positive effect on many of the young people who were sent there. All of us worked under steady pressure. Often I received calls late at night or early in the morning that required me to leave Daphne at home in order to stop a minor difficulty from becoming a major problem.

The pace tired me and left me little strength. The callus that I had tried to put out of my mind became irritated and then split open. Often during these weeks, I was able only to go to work and return to bed, as the doctor ordered, in an effort to heal the lesion. Without complaint, Daphne shouldered the responsibility of caring for me in addition to her job. Both of us found time in the evenings to continue to study the Bible and to discover what God's message to us was in this new set of trying circumstances.

The more disconcerting the problems became, the more I immersed myself in study and prayer. I met weekly with Wayne, Bud Hooper, a probation officer who worked with the Crisis Home, and Rob Ulsh, the youth director at Community Chapel. The four of us shared our experiences of trying to live Christian lives and we studied and discussed God's Word and the books we had read that interpreted that Word.

From these weekly meetings I began to examine the role of fasting as a prayer of sacrifice to God. As the pressure of the job and the continual worry about the callus increased, I fasted; sometimes for a single meal, sometimes for a full day.

My three friends became a support outside the home as strong as Daphne and the family were inside the home. Daphne and I grew even closer in our thoughts and actions as we studied together.

Despite my physical discomfort, I began in the spring of 1976 to prepare for the year's competition. Whenever I had a few spare minutes, I practiced in the lot next to the Crisis Home. One afternoon Wayne stopped to watch me. He began to offer some suggestions and to work with me. He had some excellent ideas. After several afternoons together, we agreed that he would work with me as often as our time permitted. I now had someone to help me, to watch my form, to correct me, and to help me discover ways to improve. Most importantly, Wayne provided encouragement.

Wayne was with me, as were Daphne, Mom, and Dad, as I performed at Fishersville. I don't know who was more rewarded by my performances: Dad, Wayne, or me. I set national records in the shot and in two events new to me: the club throw and the precision club throw. In the first competition I threw a wooden club, similar in shape to a small bowling pin, for distance; the second competition was for accuracy as well as distance. I also won the discus and javelin.

My next meet was the national meet on Long Island in June. Once again, the possibility of being on the U.S. team for international competition loomed. My strong performances at Fishersville and the close relationship that Wayne and I were building almost daily prompted me to think from time to time about selection to the team, the goal of every wheelchair athlete.

Selection by a National Wheelchair Athletic Association committee to participate as a United States representative in international competition was based on over-all performance in the national meet. But there were other criteria as well—the availability of housing and the availability of funds to cover the cost of the trip for the American athletes. Because the NWAA relied on contributions for the games, the size of the team varied from year to year. Sometimes as few as twenty-five athletes represented America; at other times the number swelled to fifty or more.

A series of letters back and forth from the NWAA before we left for Long Island lessened my prospect of being selected for the world games.

The first letter was from one of the U.S. team coaches. It contained information about the international Paralympics. At the bottom, it had a small typed postscript. The note asked whether I could take complete care of myself if I were selected for the international meet.

I responded that I would have no difficulty because my wife was a nurse and was accustomed to helping me with my needs.

A second letter from the coach advised me that the site for the games did not have facilities to accommodate husbands and wives. It stated that I must be prepared to take complete care of myself without assistance.

It was the second letter that increased my determination to make the team even as it reduced the possibility. I compiled an inventory of the things that I could do for myself and the things that Daphne had to do for me. I began to design solutions to my dependence on Daphne for even the smallest needs in the event that I qualified and she couldn't stay with me.

The prelude to the actual competition in Long Island could not have been more positive. Wayne and Daphne were there.
Two friends, Becky and J. K., had driven from Kentucky to be with me. Daphne and I had met Becky through Community Chapel at Virginia Beach. They had moved to Kentucky when J. K. had gotten out of the navy, but we continued to correspond.

I had all the personal support I could ask. At the outset, however, it didn't appear that their presence and support would be enough. I lost my semifinal match in table tennis and managed only a third-place bronze at the end of the first day's competition. I had learned many things from my Bible study during the past months and I was able to talk peacefully with God, asking that he help me deal with my anxieties and allow me to concentrate on my attitude.

The table tennis defeat had been erased from my mind as I prepared for the field events the next day. I knew that I was ready to do my best. I won the shot put with the longest throw ever recorded in the United States by a 1A quadriplegic. Wayne's help had paid off and it was to pay off again. I won the javelin for the first time in my career and I took a silver in the discus.

Sy Bloom, the head U.S. coach who had written the letters to me before the games, had not mentioned the Paralympics to me during the entire meet. As we waited on the final evening for him to announce the names of the U.S. team, I was certain that my achievements had eclipsed any problem about living conditions and caring for myself.

No matter how many times Sy stood before the assembled athletes, their coaches, and their friends and family on the final evening, the announcement of the members of the U.S. team was always fresh, filled with drama—having his name called was the highest accolade that an athlete could receive. It was more than recognition by one's peers in that group of special—some would say different—athletes. It was a chance to represent our country before the world and to represent every person who is disabled. It was a chance to say, "This is what we can contribute when we are provided the opportunity."

Sy explained the team selection process as his yearly preamble to the announcement of the chosen athletes. I reached for Daphne's hand.

"Daph, whatever will be, will be. Right?"

She smiled back her acknowledgement and squeezed my hand.

The audience was quiet. As each name was called, there was applause and cheering. Then silence again. Then another name and applause. At the end, there had been no applause for my name; it hadn't been called.

I looked at Daphne, then Wayne.

Wayne managed a smile. "Next year," he said and winked.

Wayne was right. It would have to be next year. I was disappointed. But I truly believed that God did not have the Paralympics in his plan for me this year.

We left the banquet hall to pack.

Just before we headed for the highway and home, we made a final stop at the hall for ice for soft drinks in a cooler.

I was amazed when Wayne came out and told me that several of the athletes were arguing with Coach Bloom about not putting me on the team.

I wanted to let him know that I hadn't initiated the lobbying effort. When I got inside, the discussion had cooled down and I had an opportunity to introduce myself to Sy Bloom. I explained that I understood his decision and that I was determined to go

home and work so hard that one day in the future he would have
to name me to the team.

I told him that even at that time, Daphne didn't have to be
constantly with me, but that I did need to have her help me with
my bowel program.

"Skip, it's a very difficult decision that we made. I wish we
could take you and some of the others. But we just don't have the
facilities available for husbands and wives at this meet."

"Coach," I told him, "I understand your decision. I just came in
to make sure you didn't think I instigated what just happened.

"I'm going home to work as hard as I can, on my events and on
taking care of myself, so that you'll have to select me one day. I
have enough faith to believe that if I'm meant to be in the world
games, I'll find a way to meet your requirements."

Sy Bloom was pleasantly surprised and impressed.

"You've certainly got the right attitude. And you've got a lot of
the right kind of faith. You're the kind of athlete we want on the
U.S. team and I believe that you're going to get there one day.
Thanks for understanding the decision."

17

Taking Inventory

We returned home from Long Island in time for Shirley's graduation from Princess Anne. She had decided to go into nursing, which really pleased me, but didn't surprise me at all. She always had been eager to help me and she seemed comfortable even with some of the distasteful little things that I required.

Several days after Shirley's graduation, a letter from Sy Bloom arrived. "There has been a cancellation by a competitor. We would like for you to be on the Paralympic team to compete in Toronto, Canada."

Preparations for my first international trip required almost as much of my time indoors as outside on the practice field.

Wayne and I worked out every other day. We focused all of our attention on my form during the practice sessions. But we avoided going all out, trying to throw for distance. That would come later when I was at the meet.

Daphne helped me try on and select the clothes I would need. Fashion had to yield to function. She sewed loops on my socks so I could get a finger through the loop and pull the socks up. She sewed large loops on the waist of my warmup pants, in the back. I practiced over and over getting dressed and undressed. Whenever I ran into a problem, we improvised a solution.

Over and over I practiced each task that I would have to master to live alone. There were the pills. And the water jug. Handling the unexpected. The invitation to the games was forcing more and more independence on me.

It was rehearsal night. I was at home and Daphne was with me. But she was not to help me this night. I was on my own.

I pushed into the bathroom, hooked my hands under my right leg and pulled it up until my foot rested on a cross-brace of the chair. Thanks to the operation on my right hand, I was able to reach down to the tube near my right ankle, unclamp it and drain my leg bag into the toilet.

I rinsed my hands and refilled my water jug at the sink. In order to drink my daily intake of a gallon and a half of water, I would have to finish another half gallon before bed.

Resting the jug in my lap, I rolled into the bedroom and pulled up to the nightstand. I reached in the drawer and pulled out a paper cup and the two rectangular plastic containers that held my pills. I opened a container. Using my thumb and the first knuckle of my little finger on my right hand, I trapped a vitamin C, raised it out of the container, and dropped it into the paper cup. Then, with the back of my index finger, I isolated each kind of pill in the second container. One by one I dropped them into the paper cup. Then I emptied the contents of the cup into my mouth and swigged long on the jug. In another five minutes I had drained the contents of the third and final jug of water.

I maneuvered the transfer board into place on the bed—the mattress was high tonight. On other nights I had practiced with it being too low. Slowly I inched my body from my chair onto the bed.

Finally I wormed myself out of my clothes, reached down for the blanket and pulled it completely over my body and head.

I had done it: the whole series of little duties and responsibilities that combined to make one night of independent living.

I pulled the blanket back from my face and grinned. Daphne smiled back at me, sharing my triumph. But the sight of her so close to me, watching every move, acting as my safety net, made my smile fade. The next time I put myself to bed, she would be thirty miles away and I would be alone.

Despite my successful practice at home, waves of apprehension washed over me as I tried to imagine what kind of facilities awaited me. Daphne would be in the building with the coaches, administrators, and family members of other athletes. Everything would have to be exactly right if I were to make it on my own.

My concentration on work at the Crisis Home and workouts with Wayne was diverted shortly before I was to leave for Canada. Karen and Rob Ulsh were married in a large ceremony in Community Chapel and the days before the wedding were filled with family activities and happiness.

It wasn't until the day before I was to leave that I realized how much I would miss Wayne's companionship and help.

"Skip, when your events start," he said before I left, "you've got to forget everything that's going on around you. The biggest thing you have to remember is to concentrate. Concentrate on what you are doing. And what you are going to do. And really explode just at the end of each throw. And follow through. When you put it all together, from start to the follow-through, that's when you get the best distances."

"I'll remember. I just wish you were going."

The scene that unfolded when Daphne and I got our first view of Olympic Village was staggering. I had never seen so many wheelchair athletes in one place. We were already tired from traveling, and the registration procedure was exhausting. Two large circus tents had been set up for registration. We went from line to line, getting medical certification for my classification, having pictures taken, receiving room assignments. I had never been exposed to something so large, so complex, and so tiring. On top of everything, the team meeting lasted until midnight.

My only thought was of rest. I had been sitting for sixteen hours. I was beginning to worry about the callus. The roll from the registration area to the dorms seemed endless. I knew that Daphne was tired, too, but I didn't have the strength to wheel myself. Finally we arrived. I was in a small single room. She unpacked for me, located my clothes where I could reach them, and kissed me good-bye. We didn't know when or where we would see each other again.

The aches in my body were soothed as soon as I was able to get myself onto the bed. I was so exhausted that I almost decided to sleep in my clothes, but I forced myself to undress, to begin to live without help.

A knock on the door awakened me. Jack Whitman, one of the U.S. coaches and a former international competitor, wheeled inside to make sure that I had gotten through the night. After he left, I managed to dress and transfer myself into my chair. What I lacked in finesse I made up for in determination. I was pleased and proud as I rolled to the door to begin the daily routine and workouts for my first international meet.

I wasn't accustomed to the demands of the practice sessions. We were up early, pushing long distances to the bus for the ride to the stadium, then sitting throughout the day as the teams worked out.

The hours of sitting in the chair took their toll. The callus on my rear split open. Before the competition started I was worn out from the demanding daily routine. I saw Daphne infrequently, the callus caused me physical and mental problems, and I had seen some of the best-conditioned athletes in the world. My sole source of strength flowed from my reading of now-familiar Scriptures and frequent prayer.

I took special refuge in Paul's words in Second Corinthians 12:10, where he explains man's weakness in relation to Christ's strength:

> That is why, for Christ's sake, I delight in weaknesses, in insults, in hardships, in persecutions, in difficulties. For when I am weak, then I am strong.

I received an emotional boost when I saw Mom and Dad on the opening day of competition. They had driven up from Virginia to be part of this event in my life. Becky and J. K. had come, too, all the way from Kentucky. The boost wasn't enough, however. As the trials for the shot put began, I realized that the athletes gathered in Toronto were, indeed, the best in the world. Their form was more polished than mine, no matter what the cause of their disability. I was deflated at the end of the trials. I was in fourth place. Dad sensed I was struggling. He came out of the stands and onto the field to encourage me. He reminded me that I was the best in the United States and that I could compete successfully with these athletes. But the tape measure told me otherwise. Just as I thought I had regained my composure, a German by the name of Weber smashed the existing world record in the shot. His throw traveled two feet farther than the best throw I had ever made. I was still in fourth place after the finals ended. No medal.

I told myself that being fourth in the world was something to be proud of, but my emotions were deaf to that reasoning. My spirits sank even lower after the discus and the club-throwing competition. I didn't reach the finals in either event.

Despite my poor showing, I was anxious to return home and start building myself. I had a much better understanding of what I needed to do to compete on the international level.

More than my renewed dedication to athletic excellence came out of the Toronto games. The opening and closing ceremonies were patterned after the pagentry that I had seen on television for the able-bodied Olympics. I was caught up in the majesty of the colors, the closing parade of athletes, and the ceremony in which the Paralympic flame was extinguished. As I watched the American flag pass in review with the flags of other countries and heard my national anthem, I found it easy to be thankful for the days I had experienced.

"Lord," I prayed, "this is not the life I chose to live, but you have shown me that my life does have a purpose. I wouldn't miss this, even the pain of defeat, for anything."

I learned two lessons from my trip to Toronto.

The first lesson dealt with my physical abilities. I knew that I had to develop more muscle and the ability to use that muscle. I changed my diet, eating balanced meals and shunning the sweet and pre-packaged snacks that had been frequent favorites.

I began to shed unneeded pounds. Wayne and I worked to transform fat into muscle. We obtained permission from Princess Anne High School to use the weight room, and we set up a schedule of weight training three days a week. Initially I started my workouts on a worn Universal Gym, using only fifty pounds in a seated military press. The first several days I had the same stiff muscles that I had known in high school athletics. I enjoyed the soreness because I recognized the feeling; it was a soreness that came from physical training. The stiffness and the aching slowly disappeared and soon we added more weight to the lift, then added new exercises to the workouts. Each increment of weight that we added proved my growing strength.

The second lesson that I learned from Toronto was more subtle; it required a lot of thought and reflection before it seeped into my mind. It dealt with spiritual growth.

Before I had gone to Canada, I had been meeting with a co-worker at the Crisis Home for Bible study. I very much respected his faith. His life was guided by daily prayer and his confidence in his relationship with God was something that I wanted to experience.

At the close of a study session together one afternoon, before I was to leave for the games, he said that he sensed, in his prayers for me, that my travel to Canada was not God's will. I was hurt and disappointed, but I know that he shared his feelings only out of love and concern for me. I talked with others, whose faith had strengthened mine, about his counsel. Their answers gave me no concrete guidance and didn't dispel my doubts about the trip and about my own faith. *Why,* I wondered, *hadn't God spoken to me in some way about the trip? Was it that I didn't truly believe in him?* I had thought, until then, that I had matured in my understanding of God.

From the moment that I had arrived in Canada, I had been confused. My confidence about my faith had been shaken. From the outset I had been plagued by disappointment. First the exhausting practices. Then the open sore. Finally, the defeats on the athletic field. Surely, from the evidence, my friend had been right.

I continued to think about the trip and its disappointments after I got home. Slowly, as I continued to study the Bible alone and with others, I began to see the trip and its events in a different light. Great benefits had come out of the trip. I had succeeded in taking care of myself without help. I had found strength in the words of the Bible when I was at a low point. I had tasted defeat in every event; yet my desire was to improve, not quit.

I began to understand that the trip had been a test for me. Out of that test and the blessings I could now see in that trip, my faith in God grew in strength and maturity. In the weeks that followed, I became excited because I knew that I was continuing to grow as a Christian. During these days of reflection and study, I committed myself to live my life to glorify God.

For many days after I made my commitment, I hoped for confirmation that my new athletic career was the way that I should glorify God. I wanted very much to remain in the world of competition. It had meant so much to me before the accident. It had given me something to strive for as I rebuilt my body. Now I felt poised to make a real contribution in wheelchair sports.

The months of training had given me strength. I now was pressing one hundred pounds, twice the amount that I had started to work with. I was mentally and emotionally ready to face the kinds of exceptional competitors who had intimidated me in Canada.

There was no quick and convenient confirmation that athletics and my commitment to God were compatible. I returned over and over to the Scriptures and to prayer. I came to realize that I would have to put my faith in God, not in myself and my own acts. I finally understood how I would receive confirmation or denial from God about continuing my athletic work.

Wayne and I had decided on a minimum of two regional meets to gain experience. Three, perhaps, if we were doing well. The trips would require considerable money; money that we did not have. In previous years, the funds had come to us in response to personal requests and as a result of newspaper articles about my efforts. I had met scores of people who had become supporters and friends and who were anxious to help me. I knew that I could call again on those who had helped in the past and we would have the finances that we needed.

But I hesitated. Something inside me made me think about what I was doing and how I was going about it. I decided not to seek the needed funds from friends. I decided to take no initiative at all in raising the money. I believed that if it were God's will that I continue in athletics, he would somehow provide the means for me to compete. I believed just as strongly that if it were his will that I turn my life in another direction to serve him, he would show me that new direction.

Often, during these weeks, I turned to Romans 8:28: "And we know that in all things God works for the good of those who love him. . . ."

I also found reinforcement for my faith in weekly meetings with my friend Bud Hooper. Rob and Wayne were no longer able to meet with us, but Bud and I continued to talk about our lives as Christians, and about Scriptures and their meanings.

I was at peace as Wayne and I continued to train.

Wayne and I had moved our workouts out of doors as the weather warmed. With the winter of weight-training behind us, the next step was to put my new strength to work in the throwing circle. At the outset of our outdoor workouts my throws were better than any of my past ones, but there was no dramatic increase.

One afternoon I was having lunch with Bob Dunsmore, the administrator for the Crisis Home system, to review my programs. A local businessman, Aubrey Perry, stopped at the table. He was a Christian and had encouraged me in wheelchair sports. The three of us chatted for a few minutes, then Mr. Perry patted me on the shoulder and started to leave. He paused.

"Skip, come by my office soon. I've got a check for you. For your traveling this year."

I was stunned.

"You do?" I knew the question sounded strange to him, but it was all that came out.

"Yes, I do." He smiled. "It will at least get you started."

I thanked him. As I spoke the words, I thanked God with all my heart. There was no question in my mind about the meaning of his gift.

Bob looked puzzled.

"Why the big smile? I've never seen you react exactly like that. You don't even know how much money he's donating for your trips."

"Bob, the amount doesn't matter," I said. "It could be five dollars, fifty dollars or five thousand dollars. I've just had a prayer answered and this is going to be a great year in wheelchair sports for me."

When I stopped by Mr. Perry's office several days later, I was given a check. A short note was attached to it. The note read, "Good luck this year. God bless." The check was for fifty dollars.

I was gripped by doubt. Maybe God's true sign would be in the form of something dramatic, a fulfillment of all my financial needs at one time.

As I drove home, my mind turned over many of the lessons I had learned in the past years in Bible study. I focused again and again on a verse in Hebrews. Finally, it filled my mind and crowded everything else out: "Now faith is being sure of what we hope for and certain of what we do not see" (11:1).

I felt it was God's way of asking me, "Don't you have enough faith to believe without evidence?" I did. The doubt subsided. I truly didn't have much evidence to believe that it was God's will that I continue in athletics. When I completed my inventory that afternoon, I had listed fifty dollars in cash and additional physical strength. But I also listed a firm faith.

Four days later, after church, Bill Taylor came over to me.

"Skip, you've got to let me know when you need the money. I've got a list of people who want to help. They're just waiting to hear from me."

I felt that God was speaking to me, saying, "You see, have the faith to believe."

The next day I telephoned Ran Randolph, the banker who had helped me with my travel funds two years before. I asked him if the account was still active. He said it was and he asked what I had in mind.

I told him only that I wanted to travel to several meets in the coming weeks and that some money had been donated for those trips. He was excited for me and told me that he would be happy to help in any way he could.

A few minutes later my phone rang. It was Ran. He asked for the details of my travel plans. I told him only where Wayne and I hoped to go.

"Skip, how are you going to raise that kind of money?"

I didn't answer his question; I was firm in my commitment not to seek help. Before I could say anything, he asked me to have lunch with him. He said he had an idea.

Ran and Jimmy Jordan, a marketing director with the bank, met me for lunch. I told them about some of my experiences in wheelchair sports and what I had learned about training since the last games. I shared with them my prayers for a Christian direction to my life.

Ran asked the question.

"Skip, have you ever spoken before a group of people? About your experiences and the accident and your faith?"

"Yes, a couple of times."

"I think you ought to be speaking to a lot of people. They would appreciate knowing about your life; it's a great example of determination and faith. Plus the sports and what you've been able to do so far. I'd like to try to arrange for you to speak to some local groups, if you're interested."

After lunch, alone in my office, I thanked God for his answer to my prayer for a sign. I felt he had shown me the direction to follow. He had led me to people who wanted to help. He had given me Ran Randolph and a way to raise funds.

Ran quickly went to work. He called the next day; he had talked with a member of the Virginia Beach Ruritan Club who wanted me to speak to that organization.

Ran, Wayne, and I, accompanied by slides of me in practice sessions, arrived on a Tuesday night for my talk.

Ran introduced me, telling the audience how he had come to know me. I prayed for God to give me the words to share with this group.

As I spoke, I sensed the attentiveness of the audience and I felt a confidence that I had never experienced before. It was a good feeling, a feeling that I was doing what I should be doing. I told my story and gave them a glimpse of wheelchair athletics. I told them I felt I could be a champion one day. It wasn't a boast. It just came out as a quiet statement. I hadn't planned to say it.

Ran closed their program by telling the club of my financial needs for travel. Before we left, Ran received a donation from the club for $250.00. Many individual members told him that they wanted to contribute, too.

One speaking engagement led to another. The newspapers picked up my story and local television stations asked me to appear before their audiences. It was an exciting time. Soon I received enough contributions to insure travel to our first regional meet. I also received acknowledgement that the way I was trying to live my life was worthwhile to others.

18

The Right Angle

The day was unusually warm for March, but a strong wind blew. Wayne and I practiced for more than two hours, and we were tired. We were also frustrated. I was a lot stronger. I could feel it every time I threw. But the new strength hadn't greatly improved my performance in any of the events.

Wayne was sitting at the foot of my chair; the equipment was spread out in front of me on the ground.

"Something's missing, Skip. Maybe I'm overlooking something," Wayne said, looking at the ground and idly pulling at blades of grass.

"I don't know. Maybe it's in my form. You know, I noticed that a lot of the athletes, some with less disability than me, sit farther forward in their chair than I do. They angle their chairs in the circle so they're throwing almost over the back of their chairs."

Wayne stopped pulling at the grass and looked up. "Say that again."

"I'll show you. Here, get up and turn my chair."

We angled the chair so that I faced almost 180 degrees away from the throwing area. I inched my body to the front of the chair.

I moved slowly through the motions of putting the shot. The new position was awkward. I had always had the left side of the chair perpendicular to the throwing area. I noticed something else, too. Even though I was putting very little pressure against the chair, the chair tipped.

"Wayne, I can't throw anything unless you hold the chair." I went through the throwing motion again and Wayne quickly saw what I meant.

"OK, let's try one and see what happens." He handed me the shot and sat on the ground, grabbing the chair with both hands and bracing it with his feet.

I threw. The shot went higher than usual, but it didn't appear to travel any farther.

I tried again. Again the shot went higher, but apparently no farther.

"Let's mark three just to see if there's any difference," Wayne said.

I put everything into the three throws. I pinned the end of the tape at the base of the chair with the javelin. Wayne reeled out the tape and walked to the spot where the first and closest shot had landed. In practice sessions, he kept the tape about waist high, eyeballed the distance and yelled it back to me. This time he eyeballed it, then kneeled down and put the tape to the ground, getting an exact measurement. He looked back with a puzzled expression, then moved to the second spot. When he looked up again, his puzzlement had been replaced by a slight smile.

He stood up after the third measurement.

"This one is over sixteen feet. They're all better than anything you've ever thrown."

"You're kidding!"

We wanted to get excited, but we couldn't believe that an adjustment in chair position would make such a difference.

I hurried through three more throws. The results were the same. Two of the throws were close to sixteen feet; the third was just over the sixteen-foot mark.

We stopped for a minute to rest and to relish what had just happened. We had the same questions on our minds: Was it chance? A fluke? Had we measured right? Could I do it again?

We moved to the discus, then the javelin. Each time I went to a new event, at least one of my efforts that March day broke a national record.

A bruise developed on my chest where it hit the back of the chair at the end of each throw, but I kept going. We worked until dark.

We practiced the next day during lunch outside the Crisis Home. We were still afraid that we would lose whatever we had found. But again, the shot throws were near or over the sixteen-foot mark.

"We've got it. We've got it, Wayne! This is the breakthrough. I can do it. I can do it consistently. We're not going to lose it," I said.

We didn't lose it. Each practice confirmed that we had reached a new plateau. There was always a feeling of relief, though, when the tape measure confirmed that I had indeed improved.

A steady cold rain fell on the Ohio State University campus in April. We waited in the van, watching the events on the field in front of us. It was the season's first regional meet. I was nervous. I kept pushing out of my mind the thought that maybe the rain or the cold would make a difference, that perhaps I could only hold my improved form in dry weather.

My first event was the javelin. At the end of my three throws, I had broken the national record by eleven inches.

The shot put was next. I threw sixteen feet, breaking the national record of fourteen feet, five inches that I had set.

I didn't set a national record in the discus, but I won that event, as well as the club throw and the precision club throw. The next day I even won the table tennis singles.

I was, to say the least, excited.

At Fishersville, with Mom and Dad in the crowd of spectators, I bettered my Ohio performances. I broke national records in the shot, the javelin, the discus, and the club. I also won the table tennis singles.

Wayne and I decided to go to a third regional, the one in New York. It would be an opportunity to gain more experience with the new form and improve my chances—if I did well—of being selected for the U.S. team.

At this point I was speaking two or three times a week to local groups, thanks to Ran's interest in me. I began to realize that people responded to my story for more than just the medals and records that were beginning to come to me.

More and more I was enjoying living my life for God. I never worked out or competed that I didn't say a quiet prayer from the Scriptures to remind myself of his blessings: "Whatever you do, work at it with all your heart, as working for the Lord, not for men . . ." (Col. 3:23).

The New York trip was going to be expensive and I was being careful about how I spent the funds that were donated. In the meantime, God was at work behind the scenes. I had met Steve Kemp at the 1976 Paralympics in Canada. Steve was a New York fireman who had been injured when he fell through a roof fighting a house fire. He had planned to compete at Long Island, but his injury turned out to be a temporary one. Now, he was recovering so rapidly that he would no longer compete in wheelchair athletics. His former sponsor offered to defray some of my travel expenses to Long Island.

As my faith grew, my view of wheelchair sports changed. I began to look on the opportunity to compete as an opportunity for anyone who was disabled to rebuild confidence in himself, as well as rebuild his body. I was proud to be part of the effort and I had pride for everyone who participated. It didn't matter to me how well someone did as long as he tried. At Eisenhower State Park on Long Island, I learned how important such an attitude could be to others in wheelchairs.

Wayne and I were studying the shot-putters as I waited for my name to be called. Some of them had to struggle to heave the shot a few precious feet from their chairs. One athlete, however, was unusually strong and agile for the 1A classification. Each time someone else's throw went only a short distance, he made a disparaging remark. I could tell it hurt some of the competitors.

His turn in the circle came before mine and his first throw was a strong one. He turned to the crowd of athletes as if to boast, "How'd you like that one?" He was good. But my heart ached for the others whom he had ridiculed. If I had needed any extra incentive, he provided it.

I knew my first throw broke a record when the shot left my hand. My body had functioned perfectly and every ounce of strength went into the throw. The official had hardly called out the distance—eighteen feet, one and a half inches—when I heard behind me, "That guy's no 1A. He's in the wrong classification." I knew who had shouted that remark. It didn't bother me. The other athletes wheeled up to congratulate me.

Wayne and I had planned to return home the next morning, but meet officials asked us to stay until the end of the competition. The reason for their request became apparent at the end of the meet. I was awarded the Alonzo Wilkins Award, given to the meet's outstanding athlete based on performance, character, and sportsmanship.

As I held the award, the athletes who had been the objects of earlier ridicule came over to me one by one. They wanted me to know that I really deserved the award.

As I looked at the award that I held in my hands, I realized that as important as it was to my increasing confidence in athletics, their words were even more satisfying.

19

An Outstanding Young Man

Soon after I returned from the New York meet, Wayne and I and three wheelchair athletes from Virginia Beach got together and formed a local wheelchair team. The four of us had competed in some of the same meets in the past, but we had entered as individuals. Wayne offered to help the other three with training and coaching. We became the founding members of the Virginia Beach Sun Wheelers. That year we went to the nationals in San Jose as a team.

At that meet, everything seemed to work for me. And there was the added motivation of a personal competition. During the 1976 national games, Fred Mcbee, an athlete from Tampa, Florida, and I had become friendly competitors. Before we left the nationals, Fred issued a friendly challenge: he was going to beat me in the shot the next time we met. San Jose was the next time.

I took first in the shot, breaking the record. Fred came in right behind me. I broke the record in the javelin. Fred was second. Then came the club throw, the final event of the meet for our 1A class. It was competition at its best. Fred made his last throw in the finals and broke the record with a toss of sixty-four feet, five inches. On my third and last throw in the finals, I hit a mark of sixty-five feet, ten inches, which beat Fred and broke the record he had just set.

Both of us had wanted the gold medal and we had pushed ourselves as hard as we could. When it was over, though, we were still friends and we were pleased for each other's performances. But,

Fred reminded me with a smile, I had a lot of work to do in table tennis before I could defeat him. He had beaten me in that event the day before to take the gold medal.

I tried to relax as Daphne and I sat at the table, waiting for the awards banquet to begin the final night in San Jose. I was at peace with myself about my performances, but still vaguely anxious. I wanted to go to the world games, but word was already out that the U.S. team would be one of the smallest in history; no more than twenty-five athletes would compete.

I was talking with Daphne when I felt a hand on my shoulder. I looked up into the smiling face of Sy Bloom. He had stopped on his way to the head table.

He leaned down close to my ear and whispered.

"Skip, can you go to England this year?"

His smile grew as he patted me on the shoulder and disappeared toward his table.

England was the site of the 1977 world games.

The door prize was a special benefit of that evening. A Roho cushion. Unfortunately, I didn't win it, but I had heard enough about it to think it could be the answer to my problem. The callus on my rear had split again during the competition. I hadn't let it affect my attitude during the games, but I didn't want to worry about it every time I competed. I left California determined to get one of those cushions.

When we landed in Denver to visit Daphne's sister and brother-in-law, Debbie and Michael Tanner, I called Roho headquarters in St. Louis, Missouri. The vice president, Otto Roberts, came on the phone to talk to me. He had read about me in *Sports 'N' Spokes,* a bimonthly magazine about wheelchair athletes, and he said that he would send me a cushion. He did.

The answer to Sy's question about England, of course, was yes.

I preceded Daphne and Wayne to England, making my first trip alone. This time Daphne was more than thirty miles away. She was an ocean away. And so was Wayne. I had come a long way that trip, in more ways than one. The first few days, though, trying to take care of all of my personal needs without Daphne's help, were vivid reminders of how very much she meant to me and how many things she did to insure my comfort.

The games began. I was defeated in the first round in singles table tennis and managed only fourth place in the discus and the club. There was no javelin throw in the world games. I won my first world medal in the shot, coming in second behind the German, Weber. Rod Vleiger, my old nemesis, and I won the gold in team table tennis, the first time I had competed in the event. It was good to be on the same side with him.

It was a rewarding meet. My marks had been consistent with my performances in the regionals. More importantly, I didn't have any trouble with the callus! The Roho cushion was the solution to an old and nagging problem.

The world games ended the year's competitions. My weekend training sessions were replaced by lazy weekends of fishing at Carolina.

Daphne and I daily gave thanks for the blessings we now had. My accident, the operations, the pain, and the fear of death all seemed so far in the past. I did not expect any greater happiness than we had. But more was to come.

The phone rang one evening and a man introduced himself to me as Pete Marx. He said he had followed my high school athletic career and had followed my efforts in wheelchair sports. He made an appointment to have lunch with me.

When I met Pete Marx, I instantly liked him. He was motivated by the joy of helping others. He asked about my background, about the accident, and how I had worked to overcome my handicaps. He wanted the Norfolk Sports Club to honor me in some way, perhaps with a special Skip Wilkins Day. I was flattered at his thoughtfulness. His interest made me realize again how much I had to be thankful for.

Weeks later the phone rang as Daphne and I were having dinner. The caller introduced himself as Rob Barton of the Virginia Beach Jaycees.

"Skip," he said, "on behalf of the Jaycees, I'd like to invite you to be our guest at a banquet on November 22nd. . . ."

I interrupted him to ask Daphne for a pen and paper. I told her that it was the Jaycees.

Rob repeated the details of time, date, and place.

"Skip, what I am about to tell you is in confidence. We haven't said anything to the papers yet."

I didn't understand what he had said or why, but I did hear and understand the next sentence.

"Skip, you have been chosen the Outstanding Young Man of Virginia Beach."

I couldn't speak. I was overwhelmed. I looked at Daphne. Tears streamed down her face. She had known all along what the call was about.

My shock gave way to joy. I had a hard time concentrating on the rest of the conversation, but I remembered clearly the names of the two people Rob said had nominated me: Bill Taylor and Pete Marx.

The Jaycees banquet was like a family reunion. Linda and Tommy, Karen and Rob, Shirley, Granny and Papa, Mom and Dad, Daphne, and I were all at one table. The room was crowded and everywhere I glanced I saw someone who had helped me, who had encouraged me on the journey back from the bottom of the lake.

Whenever I had spoken before I had not written out my speeches or made notes. I asked myself one question before I spoke: what do I want to share? And I would pray for God to provide the right words. It was like that this night, too.

As I was introduced, I silently thanked God for giving me this opportunity. So much had happened to me, so much had been done for me. Now, on this night, so close to Thanksgiving, I could give thanks in public to my family for their love and care.

I rolled to a stop in front of the podium and took the micro-phone.

"I am very honored to receive this award tonight. In accepting it, I would like to honor those who have made my life possible, because these people are what is truly outstanding in my life."

I turned to the table where my family sat.

"I was fortunate to have parents who did not panic at the time of the accident. When my life suddenly came to a halt and death was so close, they gave me hope. I am thankful to them for they made me feel accepted as I struggled to accept myself.

"I am thankful for my three sisters, who had to give up many of their wants and needs and assume the responsibilities of caring for each other and the home. When I came home, they cared for me and helped me.

"My grandparents gave of themselves, too. They taught me a great lesson in giving as they sacrificed to give me money and support to carry on a normal life.

"My wife has been always supportive and encouraging. What has been accomplished, we have accomplished together. She is truly the person who makes me complete.

"It is because of this love and the pulling together and the working together that I have been able to make something out of my life.

"There, of course, have been others who have helped me tremendously, but to try to name them all would be difficult.

"Just today, I tried to write to a person who has helped me over the past few months."

My eyes were drawn to Ran Randolph.

"This person has become a true friend, but I could not find the proper words to say on paper. But again, it is because of people caring for me that I have been allowed to achieve the things that I have.

"So, tonight, I would like to thank the Virginia Beach Jaycees for the honor of Outstanding Young Man of Virginia Beach because, by honoring me, you are really giving the honor to my family and my friends."

20

Coming Back

Ran Randolph was waiting outside my office at the Crisis Home on a cold, rainy day in February. I had been director of the home for almost three years. I had a staff of seven counselors. They cared for and provided counseling help, around the clock, for as many as fifteen children at one time.

We had successfully returned many youngsters to their homes, after helping them to calm down from an immediate crisis and to understand how to deal with future problems. Some of them couldn't adjust; others refused to help themselves. These had to be returned to the courts for further consideration. I had become accustomed to their often explosive tempers, even violence at times, but I had deep regrets when we had to return a child to the court.

I had just finished a difficult conversation with a youngster who was headed back to court for his constant aggressive behavior toward other children.

Ran was about to come into the office when a staff member stormed in, quickly became belligerent, and proceeded to complain about the salary she was paid. She was hostile and abusive. My stern reminder to her that she had been aware of the salary when she had sought the position finally dampened her anger and she returned to her duties.

On the way to lunch Ran turned to me.

"Skip, I don't see how you do it. Putting up with that kind of abuse day in, day out. You know, you have so much more to offer."

I didn't understand.

He explained what was on his mind.

"I've heard a lot of inspirational speakers, Skip. But I am moved each time I hear your story. And I've heard you speak now . . . what, about thirty times? With the gift you have, I mean speaking, perhaps a book, you could have anything you want."

I thought for a moment.

"Ran, it's not the material things. A million dollars or anything else you can name wouldn't let me walk again. What's important is what I do with what I have. I'm happy now and I have a contentment I have never known before."

"How," he asked, "can you have such a peace after what you've been through?"

"I didn't always have it. You know that. It came only when I realized that something was missing and I asked God to forgive me and to direct my life. It isn't always easy, but I feel that I'm living for him."

"I wish I had that kind of peace. There're so many things I worry about," he said.

"I can't give it to you. You have to ask for it yourself. But I can help you learn about it. All you have to do is make a commitment of time to learn with me what the Bible says about it."

Ran agreed. We discussed a schedule for Bible study and our lunch ended on a happy and thoughtful note.

Later, back in my office, I thought about Ran's comments on my speaking. I genuinely enjoyed sharing my story and the joy of my faith with others. During the past year my belief had grown stronger and stronger that God had given me a special gift in the story of my life, that it was his will that I meet with others and share his blessings on my family and me.

My spring weight training and the workouts with Wayne paid off in a big way in 1978. I won six gold medals in the regionals at Long Island. The shot, discus, club and singles table tennis continued to be my best events. The javelin had been dropped as an event, but I competed in two races and managed two firsts.

I repeated with six victories at the regionals at Fishersville. The regionals in Clearfield, Pennsylvania, brought six more gold medals.

The trip to Clearfield seemed to erase a lot of weariness and worry from Dad. He'd been able to relax and even laugh at some of the antics that Wayne and I had engaged in.

The last afternoon of the meet, Dad propped his back against the side of the van and stretched his legs out on the floor in front of him. I was lying on the backseat next to him. He surprised me when he started to talk. He'd kept so much to himself until now.

"You know, Skip, I think I'm just now getting over what we've been through. The whole family. I've never talked much about the accident, but it might help if I shared some of the things that I've tried to deal with."

He didn't wait for me to respond.

"I didn't have much of a life when I was young. No father when I really needed one. I guess I felt I had to do everything for myself. I had to prove that I was a man. That's one reason I was so stern with you when you were growing up. I wanted you to know about discipline and rules. That's part of life.

"And there's another big thing, too. You may already understand it because of what we've been through. You were my son. You were an extension of my life. You were the one person I cared about more than anyone else. Your life and athletics were everything to me. You were doing what I wished I had done when I was young.

"The accident took all of that away from me. All I had left for a while was a lot of pain and a lot of questions. But you know, I never questioned God. Not once. I used to go to the chapel in Norfolk General every time I came to see you. Nobody knows that. I didn't want them to. I'm not sure why.

"It was pretty lonely, too. I had a lot of decisions to make. And I didn't know much about what had happened to you. I mean medically. How things would turn out. A lot of the time I felt that the whole thing was on me. That nobody but me could help you. But I felt so helpless myself. It took a lot out of me. A lot more than I realized, I guess.

"But you've come back now. You'll never know what a thrill it was to watch you in the meet. I never thought we'd have these kinds of times again.

"But the most important thing I want to tell you is about the family. We need to work together to take care of the family. You never know when something might happen. Just like your accident. We've got to always be thinking what we're going to do for the family today. All of us are so important to each other."

I looked at him and nodded that I understood.

We sat in silence for a few minutes, content to be father and son. Then I began to smile. I couldn't help thinking of some of the funny things that happened as the family learned to cope with my disabilities.

"Dad, do you remember the False Alarm Caper?" This time I didn't wait for him to respond.

"Linda had brought two-year-old Kari to visit. One morning, early, Kari came into my room to see if her Uncle Skip was still asleep. I was. When she left she closed the door. It locked.

"Mom discovered the locked door when she came to awaken me.

"Loud enough to wake me up, she called, 'Skippy, you remember how we've talked about what you would do if you were alone and the house caught on fire?'

"'Yeah, Mom. Why?'

"Then she and Linda, mimicked by Kari, stood outside my door, yelling, 'Fire! Fire!'

"My chair had been left at the dresser so I snared it with the dowel rod with its saucer hook on the end and pulled it to the bedside. It took me several minutes to transfer and roll to the door.

"When I opened it, there was no fire. Only laughter.

"'I didn't know what else to do,' Mom said. 'And I thought you'd probably stay in bed all day if I told you I couldn't get in.'"

Dad, by this time, was laughing with me, so I couldn't resist telling my favorite story, the Case of Mistaken Identity.

I had gone to DePaul Hospital to visit a friend. As I rolled down the hall on the pediatric floor looking for the room, a nurse passed me.

"Young man, you'll have to get out of that chair. They're reserved for patients."

I didn't have time to explain before she continued on her way. Several minutes later, the nurse reappeared. She had another nurse with her. A large woman. Very stern.

"Young man, I'll have to insist that you get out of that chair right now. They're not for visitors to play with. They're for patients who need them."

"Nurse," I said, trying to control my laughter, "I've been trying to get out of this thing for the past four years."

The six gold medals at Clearfield were valuable. Those special moments with Dad were worth so much more.

The nationals were held at Fishersville in June. There I won three gold medals and was selected for the U.S. team that would compete in the Pan American games in Rio de Janeiro. But just as important, I received a special affirmation of my growing ministry to others.

Two months before, I had appeared on a Christian television program, "The 700 Club," hosted by Pat Robertson. On it I had told the story of my accident and the decision to give my life to the Lord.

During that meet, several athletes came to me and told me that they, too, were Christians. They had been encouraged and supported when they heard me on the program. The bonds that had tied us together, our wheelchairs and our athletics, became much stronger because of that spiritual understanding.

Before the trip to Brazil, Daphne and I went to Elizabethtown, Pennsylvania. The Fellowship of Christian Athletes had asked us to speak to their first summer conference for girls. It was Daphne's first appearance before a large group. After I had shared the story of my life, she related the story of her acceptance of God and told them something of the life of an athlete's wife. We received a standing ovation at the end of her talk, but I doubt that anyone was more appreciative of her talk than I was.

The flight to Rio with Daphne was especially enjoyable because we were leaving the United States for the first time as a couple. But considerably less enjoyable was the heat that greeted us when we arrived. It was constant and drained our strength. We soaked our T-shirts in water. Minutes later they were bone dry. I spent most of my time between events waiting in the shade under a section of the bleachers where there was often a slight breeze.

The outdoor thermometer reached 104 degrees on the morning of the shot put. I felt my strength being sapped by the heat as I waited for my turn. There was no breeze. As I made my throws, a single small cloud drifted across the sun. The sudden relief from the blazing heat brought me physical and psychological relief. I won the gold, breaking the Pan American record.

By the end of the meet, I had won another gold in the 4-by-60-meter relay, silvers in the discus and in team table tennis, and a bronze in the 60-meter race and the singles table tennis.

When Daphne and I returned to Virginia Beach, it was to a far different place than the dormitory room in Rio. Dad had built a ground-level duplex apartment next to the house for us. Mr. and Mrs. Alfred T. Wilkins, Jr., had truly come back home.

21

The Top of the Mountain

I was invited to return to the Norfolk Sports Club in late January 1979 as one of a number of local and national celebrities. We had gathered to help the club celebrate its annual day-long sports Jamboree, one of the largest in the nation. During the morning session and again at the luncheon, I was aware that the local media paid me a great deal of attention. I was puzzled by it, but as the afternoon progressed, I gave it no more thought.

That night Dad and I attended the Jamboree banquet. Wayne was unable to join us. Toward the end of the evening, I discovered why so many reporters had chatted with me and why so many of the photographers had asked me to pose with some of the national athletes in attendance.

Before Rawlings Keefe, at the head table, had finished his remarks introducing the club's Sportsman of the Year I realized, from his description, that the club was honoring me. This latest tribute gave me the opportunity to thank Wayne publically for his encouragement and help in my athletic career and to honor Dad once again for his love and determination.

No matter how many opportunities would come to me to tell others about my family's love and devotion, I knew that love and pride would well up in me each time I told of their sacrifices. That feeling of love for them became one more reason I wanted to share my life and give encouragement and inspiration to others.

The desire to build a speaking career came a step closer to reality in February. I sensed that my time at the Crisis Home was nearing an end. For four years I had worked to build the staff and to improve the facilities and the program. I felt that I had successfully met the challenges that had faced me as the home's founding director. I continued to be rewarded by the daily efforts to help the young people in our care. Each time a youngster began to open his feelings to the staff and show improved behavior, all of us shared a sense of accomplishment.

But the responsibility of shaping the home and giving it direction had largely been met.

Again, Ran was instrumental in bringing me to a big decision. He asked me to meet with Jimmy Jordan again. Jimmy had left the bank to put together, with his brother Fred, a small publishing firm in Virginia Beach. When he heard that I was thinking about leaving the Crisis Home, he asked me to consider joining the new company. He wanted me to share the story of my life in a book and he was excited about my growing interest in meeting and speaking with groups and individuals. In addition, he wanted to make time available to me to continue to compete in wheelchair games, as long as I felt there was a purpose beyond the awards. The offer seemed like an answer to my prayers about how best to use my life. I discussed the opportunity with Daphne and Dad. They, like me, thought it would be the right thing to do. I joined the firm in April and soon began to work on organizing my thoughts for a book.

Wayne and I continued our training sessions until late April when we traveled to Tampa, Florida, with other athletes on the Sun Wheelers team, for the first regional meet of the 1979 season. I was in excellent condition and the warm Florida weather was ideal. I set five Florida records, winning gold medals in the shot, discus, club, and the 60-meter and the 200-meter races. I also won the gold in singles table tennis. My shot put mark and my club throw broke national records.

The exhilaration of starting a new season with such a performance was heightened at the close of the competition when I was named Athlete of the Meet. The honor was gratifying, especially to Wayne as my coach, because the Florida meet always attracted a select group of the nation's top wheelchair athletes. I knew that Wayne and I were off to a great start and that we could have an excellent year if we didn't become overconfident.

Fishersville and Ambler, Pennsylvania, were the next regional meets. I won six gold medals in each, performing in the same events that I had in Tampa.

The nationals were held at St. Johns University on Long Island. I won the bronze medal in the 60-meters, a silver in the 4-by-60-meter relay, and a gold in singles table tennis. I broke the national record in the shot, javelin, and club and I was selected again to represent the United States in the world games.

Wayne and I began to cut back on the frequency and duration of our workouts. I needed only to maintain the physical strength that I had slowly and sometimes painfully built up during the past five years. I had never felt as well or as strong. We were both aware that I could overtrain before the world games and lose the edge that I had developed during regionals and nationals.

More important than my physical condition, as the week of the world games in England drew near, was my mental attitude. I had achieved an unparalleled record of victories during the season. Wayne and I constantly reminded each other that too much or too little confidence on my part could bring defeat in England as surely as a pulled muscle.

I viewed the 1979 world games as the top of the athletic mountain that I had been climbing. The best athletes in the world once again would challenge each other. I would face Weber again if he was still healthy and still competing. I'd never bettered him in any field event, but I had been moving closer and closer to some of his distances.

"Ladies and gentlemen," came the voice over the microphone. "Allegheny's flight one-eighty-nine for Baltimore is now ready for boarding. Please extinguish all smoking material and have your boarding passes ready for the agent. Will those passengers with

small children, passengers in wheelchairs, and anyone else needing assistance please come to the aisle on my left. We will board
you first."

Mom bent over and kissed me on the cheek. "You and Daphne
be careful. Take care. We'll be praying for you," she said. Then
she added, as always, "And have a good time."

"Do good, son," Dad said. "You know we're with you." I felt his
hand come down firmly and gently on my shoulder.

Then came Shirley. She wrapped her arms around my neck
and kissed me on both cheeks. Even at twenty she had the irre-
pressible excitement of a child.

"You all have a good time. Aren't you excited? We'll be praying
for you." All three thoughts poured out in a single stream of enthusiasm. That was just like her.

Then it was time to board.

In a short time, the plane was taxiing down the runway. We
were on our way, with Wayne and his wife, to Baltimore, then to
New York, then London. Our final destination was Wendover,
England, home of the Stoke Mandeville games, the site of the
1979 world competition.

Not long after we arrived in Wendover, I found myself sitting in
my chair, alone in the sports stadium, looking up at an engraved
message on the wall:

> The aim of the Stoke Mandeville games is to unite paralyzed
> men and women from all parts of the world in an interna-
> tional sports movement. And your spirit of true sportsman-
> ship today will give hope and inspiration to thousands of
> paralyzed people. No greater contribution can be made to
> society by the paralyzed than to help, through the medium
> of sport, to further friendship and understanding among na-
> tions.

My goal, my drive to conquer Weber, was dwarfed by the message on the wall. *The real victory,* I thought to myself, *is in the
striving, in giving my best effort.*

I remembered Dad, only hours before in the airport at home, looking down at me and speaking those three words, that benediction, as he had each time I left to compete: "Do good, son." That's what it was all about: "doing good."

It was not a typical English day. The sun had been warm at 7:30 during the announcements at the team's morning meeting. Now I could feel its heat on my shoulders as I took my place in the procession for the opening ceremonies.

The athletes, from twenty-nine countries, were an impressive sight. The brilliant colors of the uniforms and flags flashed in the midday sun.

The stadium entrance was packed with families and friends of the athletes and spectators from the neighboring towns and villages. I tried to locate Daphne in the crowd. Finally, I spotted her and she waved. As the procession of athletes began to move I looked ahead, where the coaches were grouped, and picked out Wayne.

The procession entered the stadium, moved past the reviewing stand, and came to a stop in a large formation for the opening ceremonies.

Sir Ludwig Guttmann began to speak. He recounted the history of Stoke Mandeville and the international games.

I was aware that the story we were hearing was really the story of the man who was speaking. The athletes called him Poppa—never Sir Ludwig. A German doctor, he'd gained a reputation as one of his country's finest brain surgeons. He'd come to England in 1939 as a Jewish refugee. In 1944 he opened the Spinal Injuries Center at Stoke Mandeville Hospital. Poppa had envisioned sports as a key to the rehabilitation of the war wounded.

Poppa had guided the program at Stoke. When he started in 1948, the program consisted of a few wheelchair games on the front lawn. Now it included a large indoor stadium and an Olympic-style village.

I felt a catch in my throat and swallowed hard at the words Poppa was now speaking:

"I declare the 1979 International Stoke Mandeville Games for the Physically Disabled to be open."

The strains of the British national anthem were quickly drowned out by a spontaneous cheer from the athletes.

On Wednesday, the games began in earnest for me. I faced Hans Teitze, a German, in the singles table tennis. He was good. Too good. It wasn't the hard, tactical game that I had expected to play at this level of competition. Instead, I was battling slices, curves, spins, and dink shots that just made it over the net. Junk. But it was effective. I was down 19-16, then 20-16, then the first game was over.

In the second game, I did mount a serious challenge by attacking Teitze's backhand. The German quickly compensated, though, and took the second game, 21-16, and the match.

At the end of Thursday morning's competition, I was in third place in the club throw trials, behind McCoole, an Irishman, and Weber.

I had tied the Canadian, Terwin, for fourth place in the discus—just enough to make the finals—before a noon break in the games.

That afternoon, on my way to the club finals, I mentally recapped what I had done so far in the games. A good showing, but no medal, in the individual table tennis. Not even close in lawn bowling. But then, I hadn't expected anything. Neither had Wayne. A good race, but again no medal, in the 60-meter. Now the discus was over. Still no medal. I felt that I was letting the U.S. team down. So far, I'd contributed nothing to the effort and I was holding on to only a third place in the club trials. Still to go after the club finals was the shot—my best event. And team table tennis. Then the games would be history. I had started out months ago to practice for these games. This was to be my best year ever.

Suddenly 1979 had become a fragile dream that already showed signs of cracking. I was having trouble keeping my perspective: the message on the wall to the athletes, my father's encouragement simply to "do good."

In the club throw, six athletes made the final competition. The sixth-place man finished his three tries and hadn't improved on his mark in the trials. He was out.

Only two men remained who could possibly push me out of a bronze medal. But I had to admit to myself that I was tiring from the long day and the heat. I wasn't sure I could beat my earlier throws. I waited for the indication of whether the fifth-and fourth-placed men also had been affected by the day's crowded schedule.

My answer soon came. The fifth man barely bettered his best mark in the trials, but it wasn't enough to move him up. The fourth man barely equalled his best throw of the trials. The pressure on me was swept away. I had a medal. At least a bronze. I also had a chance to upset McCoole and Weber if I could dig deep down and call up all of my remaining strength.

On my first throw, every part of my body responded to my demands. The club soared end over end. It was the best effort I could give. I bettered my mark in the trials, but I was still behind the two leaders. That first throw sapped me. My second throw was weak. The third was a solid effort, but it didn't move me ahead of my two competitors.

The club competition ended with the gold to McCoole and the silver to Weber. The bronze hung around my neck. As three of us joined hands and raised them to the crowd, I felt my confidence returning. It had been a long, tiring day. But it had ended well. I knew that I was ready for Friday, the final day. Team table tennis. And the shot.

Team table tennis was a draining experience. Each man had to play his counterpart for the best two out of three individual games, then join his teammate to play the best two out of three games in doubles. If neither side won all three matches, two more singles matches—with players switching opponents—might be required. It was necessary to win a total of three matches out of the five to advance in the competition.

My teammate was Rod Vleiger.

Because of my ranking, I played in the first match against the Irish. I beat Wheelan, a rookie, in the first two games.

Rod played McCoole. Rod pulled the first game out, but dropped the second by a narrow margin. He took McCoole more easily in the third game.

Now Rod and I faced the two Irishmen in doubles. We were two matches ahead and could advance with a win. We made short work of the first game, winning it 21-14. In the second game, we yielded to the temptation to relax and suddenly found ourselves on the bad end of a 21-19 score. That shocked us out of our complacency. We won the final game, 21-11.

Then we faced the Swiss team, the best in the world. I had wanted this. I needed to know how good I really was and how good I could become.

I drew the number one player in the world, Krumkehr. The game was a dramatic fight from the first point. Long rallies. Some almost impossible shots. The crowd constantly applauding after each point, regardless of who won it. I lost the first game, 21-18, but not my confidence. I was playing as well as I had ever played.

During the second game I attacked Krumkehr's backhand. I served first and took a one-point lead. In the next few series of serves I built the lead to two points, then to five, then to six points. And there it stayed. I beat the world champion. I needed only the next game to score an upset.

But Krumkehr demonstrated why he was number one in the world. Even in the face of the second-game defeat, he was calm and sure of his shots. The third game was the reverse of the second. It ended 21-16. But I felt like a winner, anyway. I had stayed close in the two games I lost and in one game I had beaten the best in the world.

It was time to pull for Rod now. But like me, Rod lost his first game, won the second, and lost the third. That left us two down in the overall match. We had to win two out of three games in the doubles to stay alive. In the first game, the Swiss were apparently overconfident or simply surprised by the level of our play. The game went to Rod and me, 21-16.

But the Swiss had figured out our strategy. The second game went to Switzerland, 21-17. The Swiss team led in the third game from the outset and won it, 21-18.

Rod and I were exhausted, but we were proud of what we had done. We weren't even thinking about the possibility of a medal. We were too wrapped up in reconstructing some of the shots and reminding ourselves that we had stayed all the way in the match with the world's best. So, we were caught off guard when the umpire came over to us and presented us with bronze medals. Norway had won the silver by playing in a different bracket.

Daphne walked with me to the dorm where I lay down until the loudspeaker once again summoned me to the field. The call was for the shot trials. I was calm and my thoughts were positive now. The medals had helped, but my table tennis play gave the biggest boost to my confidence. I was ready for the shot put and for Weber.

I began my ritual of competition.

As I rolled past Weber at the throwing area, I slowed for a moment. We nodded. We knew we were it—the only serious contenders for the gold. Once more the battle was between us. It was an unspoken message. Part of the ritual.

I worked my way out of my warmup jacket and hefted a practice shot. I checked the lineup. I would throw after Weber. That was a good break. Like the weather. It was still unusually warm. I rolled to a spot under the scoreboard. I had made a note of the location when Daphne and I had scouted the throwing area days before. From here I would be able to face Weber when he was in the throwing circle.

The loudspeaker called Weber's name. After his chair was locked in place with the restraining chains, the German looked out at the throwing area. I was in his line of sight; our eyes met. Then Weber turned to his work. The official handed a shot to him. He raised it several times, getting the feel of the lead ball. He nodded to the official, then settled into his throwing position, pulling the shot close to his neck. He worked the shot slowly around in his hand, seeking the most comfortable position. Then he was still. I could see his chest heave as he took the deep breath before the throw.

Weber's first try easily put him in first place in the trials. I had expected that.

Weber threw again. Slight improvement.

Then he made his final throw. I didn't look for the measurement. I kept my eyes on Weber. The German, as his chair was being unlocked, looked at me. He turned his palms up and shrugged his shoulders. I knew the body language. Weber was saying that he didn't think his throws were very good. But they were good enough. He was comfortably in first place. His best throw was 4.89 meters.

Wayne kneeled beside my chair. "I think he's holding back."

I wondered. Weber was still looking at me from the circle. I pointed a finger to my head. More sign language. Was he playing with my head? Weber shrugged his shoulders again. His chair now freed from the locking chains, he wheeled out of the circle.

"Whatta you think, Skip? You want to try to hold back some too? Or go for it?" Wayne asked.

"I'm going for it. You know that. We didn't come all the way over here to mess around," I answered.

"Good." That's all Wayne needed to say.

Several other names were called and the athletes went through their throws. I recognized most of them. It was hard to believe that I'd been competing in wheelchair sports for six years now.

"Wilkins, U.S.A.," the voice summoned over the loud-speaker.

As I rolled toward the throwing area, I concentrated on what Wayne and I would have to do in the next several minutes. The precise chair angle came first. Then Wayne's exacting preparations to anchor the chair. Then the selection of the better shot. The deep breaths. The concentration. The lunge forward. The extension of my arm. The release. Each step had to be perfect. *Each will be,* I told myself. *They'll* have to be, *if I'm to beat Weber.*

Wayne and I entered the throwing circle. We received the approving nod of the official for Wayne to help adjust the chair. I worked it into the proper position, facing away from the field.

The official looked at his watch, then gave Wayne the sign that he and I could no longer communicate. I made the last, slight adjustment to the chair and Wayne carefully tightened down the chains, two on each side. Wayne had performed this act for me hundreds of times, but he always worked as slowly, as patiently, as carefully as he had the very first time. He knew that even a slight movement of the chair could affect my effort.

The official entered the circle, a shot in each hand. The weight of the first shot startled me. It weighed slightly more than the two kilos I had used in practice. Not much more, but enough to feel strange in my hand. It was an unwelcome surprise. I hefted it several more times, trying to adjust to the weight. I returned it and took the second shot. It, too, felt heavier than two kilos, but it was lighter than the first. That happened. No two shots were identical. I nodded to the official who retreated with the first shot.

I inched my torso toward the front of the chair, reached my left hand behind the left chair handle, and hooked my thumb beneath the handle. I positioned the shot more comfortably in my hand and tucked it under my chin.

Come on, Skip. This is it, I told myself. I felt the muscles in my left arm tighten all the way down to my thumb, hooked beneath the chair handle. In one motion, I pulled my body toward the throwing area with my left arm, thrust my right arm up and out, and released the shot. It was a good, clean throw, but I didn't think that it traveled far enough to dislodge Weber from first place. The crowd's reaction told me otherwise when the shot thudded to the ground. The second throw felt good, and I knew the third shot had to be close to Weber's distance.

I rolled out of the circle.

"What's your best mark?" the official asked. Before I could recall the figure, my marks were called over the loudspeaker.

"Wilkins. U.S.A. First throw, 4.92 meters. Second throw, 5.09. Third throw, 5.12."

It wasn't a personal record, but it was more than enough for the trials.

I was in first place. Two-tenths of a meter in front of Weber. I did some quick conversion math. That was about nine inches. It was a solid difference if Weber had given his throws everything that he could. The roles were reversed for the first time. Weber had to catch me now. Had he held back? If so, how much had he saved for the finals?

I rolled to a shaded area and watched the remaining five competitors. None came close to my last throw.

I headed for the dorm and rest, but sleep wouldn't come quickly. I tried to force my mind to slow down, but it wouldn't. It kept toying with the prospect of winning the world title. For a while, I gave up trying to suppress the thought. It was too pleasant. But I knew it was dangerous. *Don't start wearing medals before you win them,* I said to myself.

Wayne's voice brought me out of my sleep. It was 4:40 P.M. Time for the last test of this 1979 season. A large crowd had gathered for the finals. Athletes from every country were lined behind the circle. There were only four finalists in the event. My three competitors were already working with their coaches to stretch and warm their muscles. Weber and I again exchanged nods. I found a spot out of sight from the throwing circle. Weber would have to apply the pressure this time.

The fourth-place man was in the circle, beginning to position himself for his first throw. As I watched him, a strange and illogical possibility broke my thought of becoming number one in the world: suppose the fourth-place or the third-place man had been holding back? Suppose one of them beat Weber and me? I watched the shot as it left the thrower's hand and began its arc. Before it landed I knew that the fourth-place man might move up one position, but would not come close to Weber or me. The second throw, then the third, followed the arc of the first and landed within inches of his first effort. He hadn't improved his standing.

Now the third man began positioning for his first throw. Again I thought the improbable. Suppose? But there wasn't any supposing. He improved his own mark slightly, but remained well behind me.

I tried to remain calm, but I couldn't. Daphne rested her arm across my shoulder. I reached up and rested my hand on hers. But I could feel my excitement building.

Weber was in the circle, taking a lot of time to get his chair positioned.

"Hurry up," I whispered under my breath. I was anxious. I wanted to know immediately how much better I would have to throw to beat the German. Weber's first throw was a poor one. *Maybe he didn't hold back,* I started to tell myself. But I knew better. Weber had been too anxious on the first throw and had released too soon. The throw was well behind his distance in the trials.

It seemed that hours passed as Weber readied for his second throw. I squirmed in my chair. The whole area was silent. Weber launched his second throw. It was not a long one. Again Weber had let the shot go an instant too soon. I knew from my own experience that the pressure was a big factor. Weber had to know, before that second throw, that he had only two chances to keep his title. Now he had only one.

My mouth went dry. I wanted to call out, yell, do anything to break the tension. I wasn't sure I could watch the last throw. It could mean as much to me as it did to Weber. I wanted to turn away, to avoid the possible sight of the shot soaring beyond my ability to match it or to beat it. But my competitive instincts overpowered my nerves.

Weber leaned forward, brought his weight to the back of the chair, snapped his body forward, and extended his arm. The throw looked good. The crowd sighed in admiration as the shot reached the highest point of its flight.

"That's the big one," I said in Wayne's direction. I hefted a shot in my right arm.

When Wayne didn't respond, I looked at him. Suddenly he started jumping up and down and grinning.

"You've done it. You've beaten him!"

I turned toward the head official. The figures were being called out for Weber's last throw. "Weber. West Germany. 4.91 meters."

It was over. I was the world champion in the shot put. I could feel tears come to my eyes. I swallowed and smiled. More tears came. Daphne was leaning down, hugging me. She was crying, too. We looked at each other, then at Wayne. It was our moment. It had been a long time in coming.

The official hung the gold medal around my neck. I caught my breath when the "Star-Spangled Banner" began. For the first time since the accident I felt that I had come back. All the way back. With God's help and my family's love. I knew nothing was impossible for me now.

22

A Heck of a Life

Speaking invitations awaited me when we returned from England. Many of them had resulted from the local newspaper and television reports of my performance at Stoke Mandeville. I was especially pleased at the requests that had come as a result of earlier talks I had given; people were telling their friends and acquaintances about me and the message I wanted to convey.

I was thankful for the joys that I was experiencing and for the ability that God had given me to touch others.

Wayne and I further refined my training program. I spent more time in weight training and less time on the practice field in the early weeks of the next season. As the first regionals, again in Florida, approached, we discontinued the workouts with weights and began to work on my form. We rarely put a tape to the throws. We concentrated on the almost imperceptible shifts of my body in the chair, always striving for just a little more leverage that would add precious distance to my efforts.

Our efforts paid off.

The 1980 nationals were held at the University of Illinois in Champaign-Urbana. There, for the first time during any of my meets, I met with other athletes for morning Bible study. We gathered, beginning the first day, on the lawn of the campus to exchange our experiences and to learn more about the Scriptures.

On the second morning of our study, one of the athletes told us he had found personal strength and purpose in several verses from a chapter in First Corinthians:

> Do you not know that in a race all the runners run, but only one gets the prize? Run in such a way as to get the prize. Everyone who competes in the games goes into strict training. They do it to get a crown that will not last; but we do it to get a crown that will last forever. Therefore I do not run like a man running aimlessly; I do not fight like a man beating the air. No, I beat my body and make it my slave so that after I have preached to others, I myself will not be disqualified for the prize (9:24-27).

The verses made a deep impression on me as I reread them that night. I read them over and over during the meet. That was what it was all about. Running the real race. Receiving a crown that will last forever. A crown that was far more important than all the gold medals I had won or would win.

Daphne traveled with Wayne and me to the nationals. As we finished breakfast on Sunday, the day of the finals, I couldn't help but be pleased. It had been a good meet for me. I had narrowly beaten my first table tennis opponent on the opening day, but I settled down and won the event. At the end of the trials on Saturday, I was in first place in the shot put, discus, and club, the only track and field events that I had entered.

When competition resumed, I held onto my first place in the shot and then the discus, adding two more gold medals.

My first club throw was a strong one. It landed 21.85 meters from the circle, a new national record. My second and third throws also shattered the record; the longest soared 23.23 meters.

I won a gold in every event I entered.

It was only as we finished our banquet dinner that my emotions began to subside. The after-dinner conversation dropped to a murmer, then died. Cliff Crase, the editor of *Sports 'N' Spokes*, began to address the audience of athletes, coaches, husbands, and wives.

He was highlighting the career of Jack Gerhardt, an earlier wheelchair athlete. I knew from previous banquets that Jack Gerhardt had been a leader in the United States on behalf of the disabled. He had been in the forefront of organizing athletic competition for those in wheelchairs. As a result of his efforts, he had been featured on the cover of *Newsweek* magazine in 1932. An award, named for him, was given annually to the U.S. Athlete of the Year.

"This year," Cliff Crase said, as he began to introduce the award winner, "the award goes to a person who's been around in this competition for six years. This person holds a host of national records in wheelchair competition. . . ."

Cliff's voice trailed off and the attention of the crowd, including Daphne's and mine, became more intense.

"I think perhaps the best thing I can say about this year's winner is to tell you that I just plain like him. And so do you. Skip Wilkins."

I was in a state of shock. So was Daphne. Neither of us could say a word. We just looked at each other with wide eyes. Her mouth was open. I guess mine was, too. It took several seconds even to hear the applause and to realize that everyone was looking in my direction, clapping and cheering. Those who were able to stand were on their feet.

I don't remember who pushed my chair up the incline and onto the dais. I was at a loss for words. Cliff handed me the plaque and shook my hand.

But when I turned my chair to face the audience, I found that I was no longer at a loss for words. What I felt and what I wanted to share with these people, my peers and my friends, came from every part of my being.

"This is truly unbelievable," I began.

"There are so many of you who deserve this so much more; who have competed successfully so much longer. It belongs as much to each of you as it does to me. You have helped me and encouraged me to become what I am in wheelchair sports.

"Awards like this one are not possible without other people. I'm fortunate to have a committed coach who could make an award like this possible.

"I've been blessed, too, with the love and support of a family who wouldn't let me quit when things got a little tough.

"And then there's my wife, Daphne. You know her. She's the one who's nursed me through the aches and the pains of trying, of learning, and of always seeking to improve. She's been with me in everything that I've tried to do and she's always waiting for me—after the long practice sessions and the trips away from home when she can't go with me."

I turned toward the head table.

"And, of course, there's you. The people who, year after year, make this possible for all of us."

Then I looked at the people spread out in front of me.

"You know, there are very few of us in this room who chose or planned the kind of life we now lead. But once we've accepted our lives and once we're willing to do something with them, it really can be *a heck of a life*."

I turned to roll off the platform. Wayne, with tears in his eyes, came up to hug me and to take the chair and guide me back to the table.

Fellow athletes and friends, old and new, reached out to shake my hand and to pat me on the back as Wayne guided me through the maze of tables.

As the audience slowly began to turn its attention back to the head table, Sy Bloom made his way toward the microphone.

As he always did, he spoke slowly and carefully. He wanted everyone in the audience to understand how the members of the U.S. team were selected to compete in the world games.

He finished the explanation and his normally soft voice rose slightly.

"It's always a privilege," he said, "and it gives me great pleasure now to introduce those athletes who have been selected to represent the United States of America in Arnhem, Holland, in the 1980 Paralympics."

Sy Bloom looked down at the sheet of paper in his hands. He spoke with a strong voice as he began to call the roll of athletes.

"Skip Wilkins . . ."

1951: Tommy and Patsy with Skip, 1½, and Linda, 3 months, in a family portrait.

1959: Granny and Shirley, Papa and Karen, Skip, 10, and Linda, 8, at the traditional family breakfast on Christmas Day.
1961: Skip, 12, with the first bass he caught with a new rod and reel.

HIGH SCHOOL:

1965: Skip, 16, as a halfback for Princess Anne High School in a game against Craddock High in his junior year.

1967: Skip, 17, on an early spring day after surfboarding.

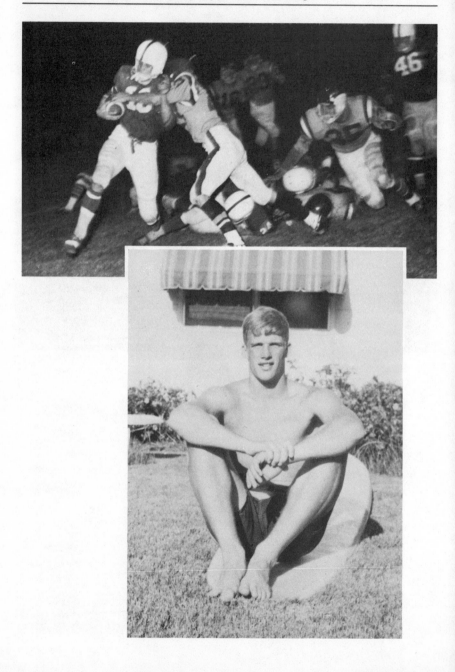

ACCIDENT:

1967: Skip in Norfolk General Hospital just days after the accident.
1967: Skip on his first day at Woodrow Wilson Rehabilitation Center.

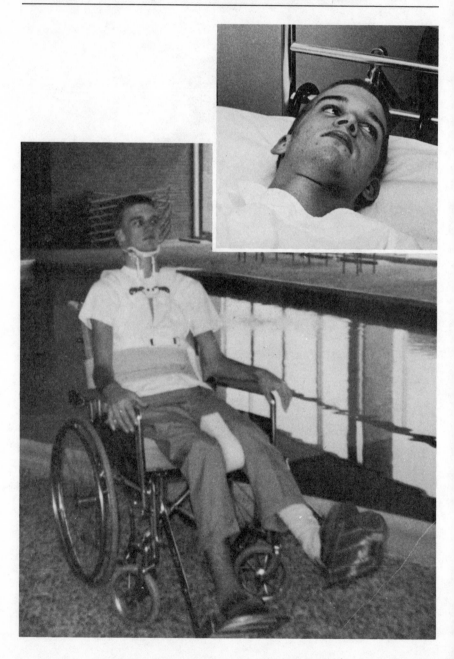

1967: Skip, 18, with Shirley, Karen, Linda and his dad at home for a Christmas visit from Woodrow Wilson.

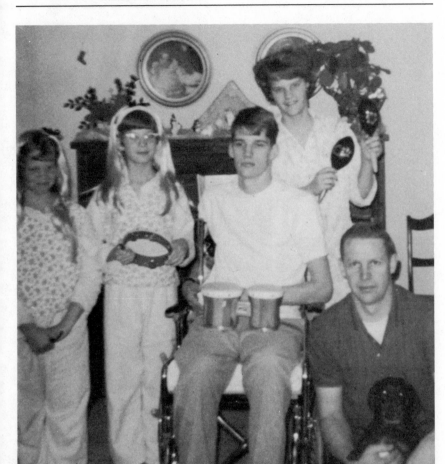

NEW BEGINNINGS:
1970: Skip and Daphne on a summer afternoon in the back yard.
1972: The wedding party at Berea Baptist Church: Mary Bradley, sister Linda, Daphne, Skip, Linda's husband Tommy Viar, and Paul Bradley.

1978: Skip and his dad after a track meet in Clearfield, Pennsylvania.
1978: Skip, in a specially designed chair, at the helm of his boat.

ATHLETICS:

1979: Skip at the start of his throw in the shot-put finals at Stoke Mandeville, England.

1979: Wayne Whitley and Skip after winning the gold medal in the shot in England.

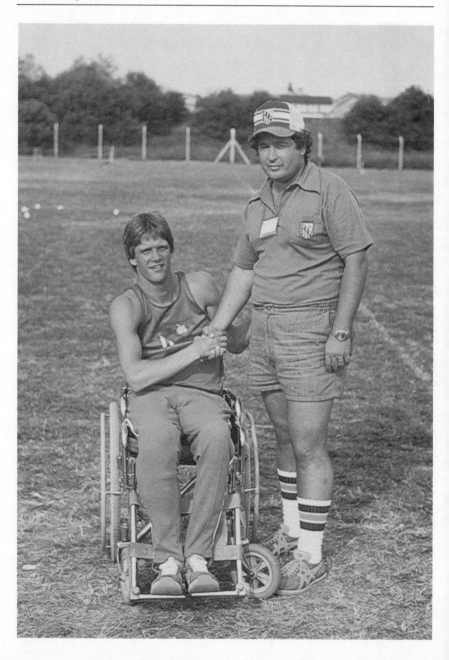

1980: Skip during a talk to community league football players.

1980: Karen, Linda, Skip, Daphne, Shirley, Patsy and Tommy in the Skip Wilkins' home at Christmas.